W9-CET-975

Facts about
Germany

CONTENTS

FOREWORD

What characterises politics, business, society, academia, and culture in Germany? "Facts about Germany" invites readers to get to know the modern and cosmopolitan country. The handbook offers exhaustive basic information and numerous points of orientation – all specially designed with international readers in mind.

In nine chapters, "Facts" conveys a basic understanding of German society and shows which models and solutions are being discussed in a time of social and political change. The new 2018 edition focusses in particular on contemporary issues – historical and institutional references take a backseat. In order to make the texts as useful as possible, they include up-to-date information and statistics.

The print edition of "Facts about Germany" includes broad digital offerings, exploring in more depth online the topics outlined in the print edition. ■

Get to know Germany – with the cross-media "Facts about Germany"

FACTS FAMILY

Insight: Informative overviews spotlight current developments in the topic explored in each chapter.

Topic: Fact-based texts offer an in-depth and expanded consideration of the key aspects.

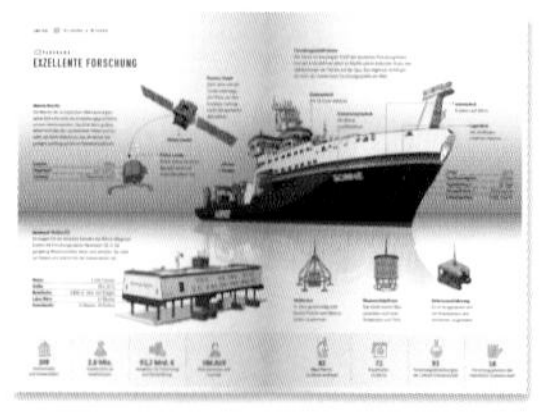

Panorama: Extensive info graphics complement the chapters, adding an exciting visual component.

HANDBOOK

In its nine chapters the updated edition of the handbook "Facts about Germany" offers a whole host of different angles on present-day Germany. Each of the chapters is structured in such a way that an "Insight" first provides the most important basic information on the topic in question by way of introduction. Subsequently, the various aspects of the topic are explored in depth. Moreover, each chapter contains numerous references to further sources of information as well as cross-media services.

- → **Information in 14 languages**
- → **Nine chapters**
- → **Various information levels**
- → **Tips for further information**
- → **Key players in each topic**
- → **Print-to-Web links via augmented reality applications**

MORE ABOUT GERMANY

Anyone wanting to find out more about politics and business, about culture, science, and society can rely on the Deutschland.de website. Here you will find the stories behind the stories in the news and access to contacts who can provide the right information on topics

facts-about-germany.de:
Modern design meets concentrated information.

DIGITAL

Pride of place in the extensive multimedia digital offerings goes to the website **facts-about-germany.de**. What is more, the responsive design enables optimum use on mobile end devices. The "Facts" range also includes e-paper editions and e-reader services. The facts-about-germany.de website won the German Design Council's German Design Award 2018 in the category "Excellent Communications Design – Online Publications".

VIDEO AR APP

Additional digital material

1. Download the free app "AR Kiosk" from your app store onto your mobile device. "AR Kiosk" is available from iTunes and Google Play.

2. Start the app and hold your smartphone or tablet over the image with the icon Video & AR app (pages 23, 39, 59, 79, 95, 115, 135, 155). Additional digital information is available via these pages.

3. As soon as the app has recognised the image, the bonus material will automatically open.

→ Information in 14 languages
→ Videos and interactive graphics
→ Additional chapter "German History"
→ Extensive background information and in-depth key words on each chapter

such as studying, working, or travelling. The website also casts a regional glance at the topics and people linking Germany and its partners around the world – in contributions for ten world regions. And feel free to interact with Germany on social media channels.

deutschland.de
facebook.com/deutschland.de
twitter.com/en_germany
instagram.com/deutschland_de

AT A GLANCE

Federal Republic • Crests & Symbols • Demographics • Geography & Climate • Parliament & Parties • Political System • Federal Government • Famous Germans

FEDERAL REPUBLIC

Germany is a federation. The federation and the 16 Länder (states) each have areas of responsibility of their own. Responsibility for internal security, schools, universities, culture, and municipal administration lies with the states. The administrative authorities of the states enforce not only their own laws, but also those of the federation. Through their representatives in the Bundesrat the governments of the states are directly involved in the federation's legislation.

Federalism in Germany is more than just a system of federal states; it represents the country's decentral cultural and economic structure and is deeply rooted in tradition. Over and above their political function, the states are also a reflection of pronounced regional identities. The strong position of the states was established in the Basic Law in 1949; on reunification in 1990, five new states were founded: Brandenburg, Mecklenburg-West Pomerania, Saxony, Saxony-Anhalt, and Thuringia. With 17.9 million inhabitants, North Rhine-Westphalia is the most populous state, while its 70,540 square kilometres make Bavaria the largest in terms of surface area; with 4,012 inhabitants per square kilometre Berlin, the capital, is the most densely populated. There is one peculiarity: the three city states. Their territory is restricted in each case to a major city, namely Berlin, Bremen/Bremerhaven, and Hamburg. With 420 square kilometres and 679,000 inhabitants, Bremen is the smallest state. Economically speaking, Baden-Wurttemberg is one of the strongest regions in Europe. After the Second World War, Saarland was a partly sovereign state and a French protectorate, and was only integrated in the former territory of the Federal Republic as the tenth state on 1 January 1957. ■

The 16 federal states

Federal Eagle

The Federal Eagle is the German state symbol that is the richest in tradition. The Federal President, the Bundesrat, the Federal Constitutional Court, and the Bundestag use differently styled eagles. The eagles that appear on coins and the national strip of German sports associations also differ in terms of design.

Basic Law

Passed in 1949 in Bonn, the Basic Law was initially intended to be provisional. After reunification in 1990 the version was then adopted as the permanent constitution. The 146 Articles of the Basic Law supersede all other German legal norms and define the basic systems and values of the state.

Flag

The Basic Law states that the colours of the federal flag shall be black, red, and gold. In 1949, this followed on from the flag of the first German republic of 1919. The Nazis had abolished the latter and replaced it with the swastika.

National Holiday

As the Day of German Unity, in the Unification Treaty of 1990 3 October was declared a national holiday in Germany. The Day of German Unity is the only national holiday to be determined by federal law.

Currency

The euro has been the legal tender in Germany since 1 January 2002. It replaced the deutschmark, which had been in use since 1948. The European Central Bank (ECB) is headquartered in the German financial centre Frankfurt am Main.

Domain

The domain ".de" is the most widespread country-specific domain in Germany, and the most popular worldwide. Using the international dialling code +49, 99.9 percent of households can be reached via landline or mobile telephone.

National Anthem

The German national anthem consists only of the third stanza of the Deutschlandlied by August Heinrich Hoffmann von Fallersleben (1841). The melody was written by Joseph Haydn in 1796-97.

DEMOGRAPHICS

With regard to demographic developments there are three clear trends in Germany: a low birth rate, rising life expectancy, and an aging society. With 1.36 million babies born, Germany registered its highest birth rate in 1964, since when the country has been at a low as far as births are concerned. In 2016 however the number of new babies born rose for the fifth year in a row; with a birth rate of 1.59 children per woman, Germany moved into the European statistical midfield. Nonetheless, for 35 years the generation of children has been about a third smaller than that of its parents – nowadays there are twice as many 50-year-olds as there are newborn babies. At the same time, life expectancy is rising. For men it is on average 78 years, for women 83 years.

The demographic changes and the serious impact they have on economic development and the welfare systems are being cushioned by immigration. Just over 22 percent of the people living in Germany (18.6 million) have a migration background. More than half of them have a German passport. Members of four national minorities are recognised as having long-established roots and enjoy special protection and support: the Danish minority (50,000) and the Friesian ethnic group (60,000) in north Germany, the Lusatian Sorbs (60,000) along the German-Polish border, and the German Sinti and Roma (70,000). ■

LIFE EXPECTANCY

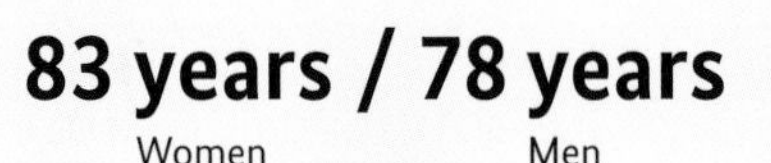

Women Men

IMMIGRANTS IN 2016

1,865,000

EMIGRANTS IN 2016

1,365,000

HOUSEHOLDS

40.8 m

POPULATION

82.6 m

GENDER DISTRIBUTION

40.74 m
Women

41.83 m
Men

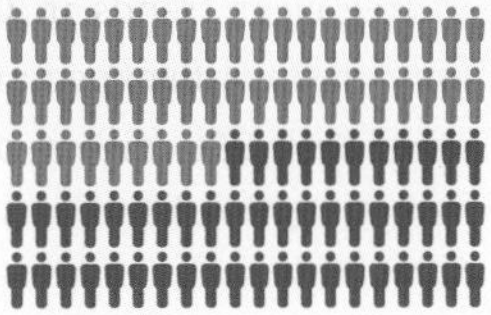

AGE STRUCTURE

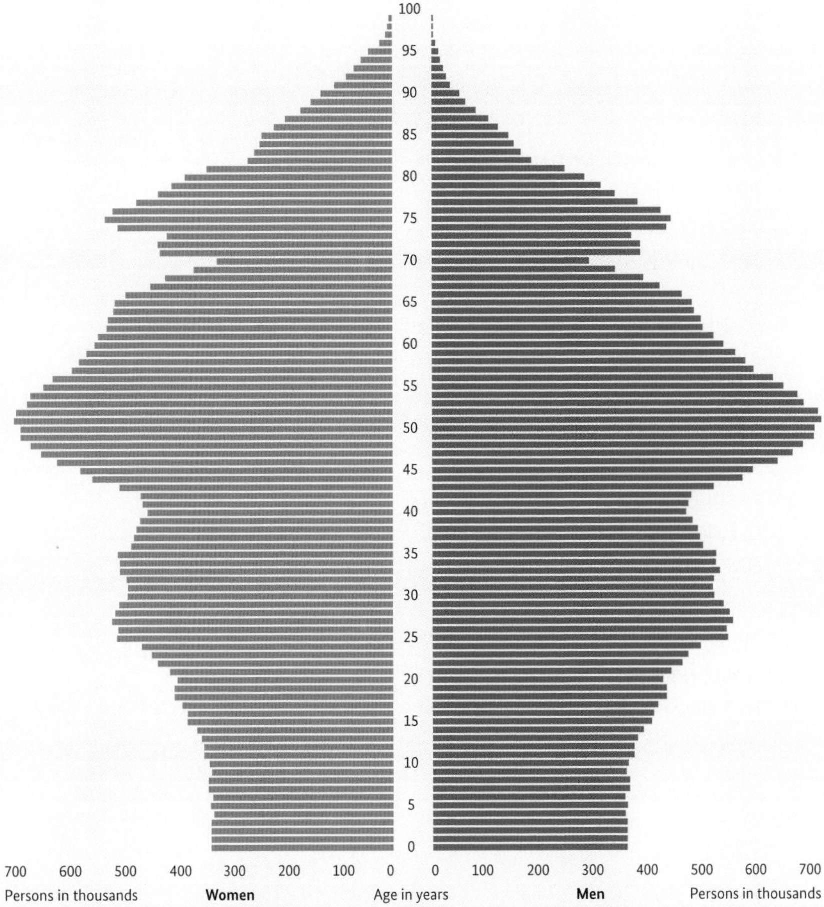

100
95
90
85
80
75
70
65
60
55
50
45
40
35
30
25
20
15
10
5
0

700 600 500 400 300 200 100 0
Persons in thousands **Women**

Age in years

0 100 200 300 400 500 600 700
Men Persons in thousands

Source: Federal Statistical Office

GEOGRAPHY & CLIMATE

Germany lies at the heart of Europe. It shares its borders with nine other nations. No other European country has more neighbours. In the north, Germany has access to the North and Baltic Seas. In the south it borders on the Alps. At 2,962 metres the Zugspitze in Bavaria is its highest peak. At 3.54 metres below sea level the lowest point on land is near Neuendorf-Sachsenbande in Schleswig-Holstein. Measuring 357,340 square kilometres, Germany is the fourth largest country in the European Union (EU) after France, Spain, and Sweden. Forests cover almost a third of its total surface area. Lakes, rivers, and other inland waters account for more than two percent. The Rhine is the longest river. In the southwest it marks the border between Germany and France, further north Bonn, Cologne, and Düsseldorf all lie on its banks. The Elbe, the second-longest river, links Dresden, Magdeburg, and Hamburg and flows into the North Sea.

Germany enjoys a moderate climate. In July, the mean maximum temperature is 21.8 degrees Celsius, the minimum 12.3 degrees. In January, the mean maximum is 2.1 degrees, the minimum –2.8 degrees. The highest temperature since records began was recorded on 5 July 2015 in Kitzingen am Main, namely 40.3 degrees Celsius. ■

LOCATION

Central Europe

SURFACE AREA

357,340 km²

CAPITAL

Berlin

891.70 km²

HOURS OF SUN

1,595

RAIN

850 l/m²

COASTLINE

2,442 km

LONGEST RIVER

Rhine

865 km in Germany

FORESTED AREA

114,191 km²

HIGHEST MOUNTAIN

Zugspitze

2,962 m

PARLIAMENT & PARTIES

The German Bundestag is elected every four years by free, secret, and direct ballot by citizens aged 18 and over who are eligible to vote. The Bundestag is the German parliament. Half of the at least 598 seats in the Bundestag are allocated through the election of candidates put up by the parties on state lists (second votes), the other half through the election of persons in 299 constituencies (first votes). The German electoral system makes it difficult for any one party to form a government on its own – meaning that a coalition tends to be the rule. In order to prevent complications in the formation of majorities by the presence of small and very small parties, a threshold known as "the five percent hurdle" excludes parties that poll less than that being represented in the Bundestag. Seven parties with 709 members of parliament are represented in the 19th Bundestag: CDU, CSU, SPD, AfD, FDP, The Left party, and Alliance 90/The Greens. Ever since the first Bundestag election in 1949, the CDU and its sister party CSU, which only stands in Bavaria, have formed a single parliamentary party. Alternative for Germany (AfD) entered parliament for the first time in this legislative period; the FDP is once again represented in the Bundestag after a four-year break. The current Federal Government is made up of a coalition of CDU/CSU and SPD, with Dr. Angela Merkel (CDU) as the Federal Chancellor, Olaf Scholz (SPD) as Deputy Chancellor and Heiko Maas (SPD) as Federal Foreign Minister. AfD, FDP, The Left party and the Greens form the parliamentary opposition. ■

Parties

CDU

Christian Democratic Union of Germany (CDU)
427,173 members
2017 election result: 26.8 percent

Social Democratic Party of Germany (SPD)
463,723 members
2017 election result: 20.5 percent

Alternative for Germany (AfD)
29,000 members
2017 election result: 12.6 percent

Freie Demokraten FDP

Free Democratic Party (FDP)
63,050 members
2017 election result: 10.7 percent

DIE LINKE.

The Left party
62,182 members
2017 election result: 9.2 percent

Alliance 90 / The Greens
65,257 members
2017 election result: 8.9 percent

Christian Social Union (CSU)
141,000 members
2017 election result: 6.2 percent

Bundestag

The Bundestag has at least 598 members. In addition, there tend to be what are known as “overhang and equalising” seats. The 19th Bundestag as elected in 2017 has 709 members.

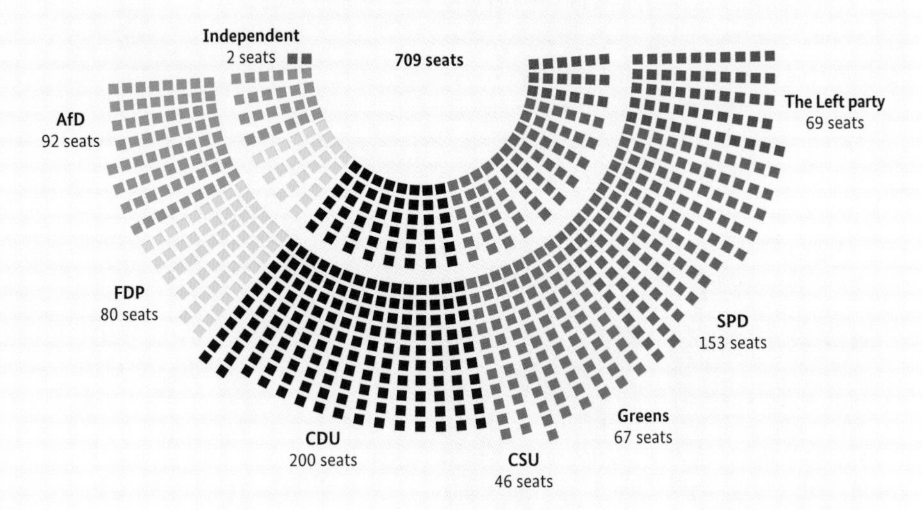

Bundesrat

The Bundesrat is one of five permanent constitutional bodies. It represents the Länder, the federal states. The Bundesrat is made up of 69 representatives of the state governments. Each state has at least three, the most populous state up to six votes.

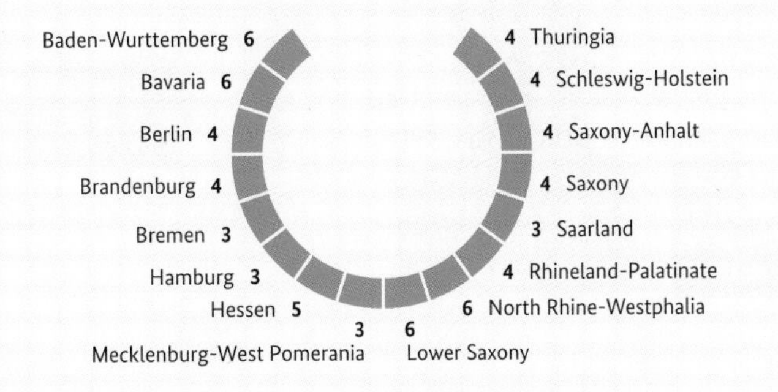

POLITICAL SYSTEM

In terms of protocol, the Federal President is Germany's most senior representative. The President of the Bundestag is, in terms of protocol, the second most senior. The proxy for the Federal President is the President of the Bundesrat – an office held on an annual basis by the premier of the one of the federal states. The office with the greatest political power is that of the Federal Chancellor. The President of the Federal Constitutional Court is likewise one of the country's high representatives. ■

Dr. Frank-Walter Steinmeier, b. 1956, Federal President since March 2017

Dr. Angela Merkel, b. 1954, CDU, Federal Chancellor since November 2005

Dr. Wolfgang Schäuble, b. 1942, CDU, Bundestag President since 2017

Dr. Andreas Vosskuhle, b. 1963, President of the Federal Constitutional Court

The people

All German citizens aged 18 and over are eligible to vote. They elect MPs in a general, direct, free, and equal election by secret ballot.

elect

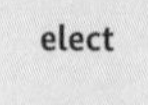

elect

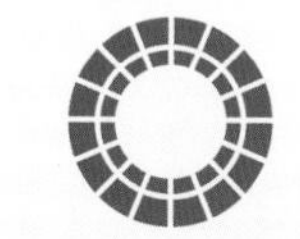

State parliaments

As a rule the legislature of the state parliaments is five years. The state constitutions regulate their powers and how they are organised.

send delegates to

elect

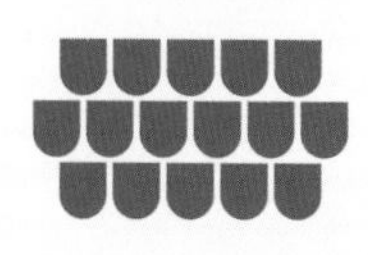

State governments

The state governments are elected in each case by the state parliaments in a secret vote, and can also be brought down by them.

send delegates to

The Bundestag

The parliament is elected for four years and has 598 members. In addition there are so-called overhang and equalising seats. The Bundestag is responsible for legislation and monitoring government.

elects

The Federal Chancellor

The Chancellor is elected by the Bundestag in a secret vote. The Chancellor determines policy guidelines and is head of the Cabinet.

proposes

The Federal Government

The government comprises the Federal Chancellor and the federal ministers. Each minister runs his or her ministry independently.

elects

sends delegates to

The Federal Assembly

The Federal Assembly convenes solely for the purpose of electing the Federal President, whom it elects in a secret vote for a five-year term of office.

appoints

appoints

elects

The Federal President

The head of state's duties are primarily of a representative nature and he represents the Federal Republic in international matters. He appoints the Chancellor and the federal ministers and issues laws.

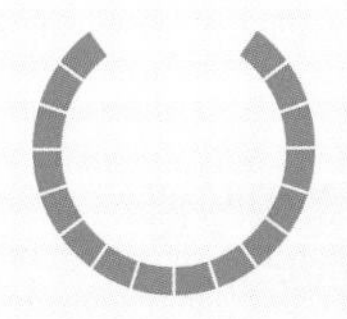

The Bundesrat

The chamber of states is made up of 69 members delegated by the state governments. In many fields laws require the approval of the Bundesrat.

elects

elects

Federal Constitutional Court

The Court has 16 judges. Half of them are elected with a two-thirds majority by the Bundestag and Bundesrat.

FEDERAL GOVERNMENT

The Federal Chancellor and the federal ministers form the Federal Government, the cabinet. Alongside the Chancellor's power to set policy guidelines, within these general parameters ministers on principle run their ministries independently; the collective principle also applies, whereby the Federal Government settles disputes by majority decision. The federal cabinet consists of 14 ministers and the Head of the Federal Chancellery. The federal ministries are the highest federal authorities for the relevant departments. The Basic Law assigns the Chancellor a special role: "The Federal Chancellor shall determine and be responsible for the general guidelines of policy." The Federal Chancellery and the federal ministries employ around 18,000 staff members. The Federal Foreign Office and the Federal Ministry of Defence are among the ministries with large payrolls. Eight ministries are based in Berlin, six in the Federal City of Bonn. All the ministries maintain offices in both cities. ■

Federal Ministries

Federal Ministry of Finance
→ **bundesfinanzministerium.de**

Federal Ministry of the Interior, Building and Community
→ **bmi.bund.de**

Federal Foreign Office
→ **diplo.de**

Federal Ministry for Economic Affairs and Energy
→ **bmwi.de**

Federal Ministry of Justice and Consumer Protection
→ **bmjv.de**

Federal Ministry of Labour and Social Affairs
→ **bmas.de**

Federal Ministry of Food and Agriculture
→ **bmel.de**

Federal Ministry of Defence
→ **bmvg.de**

Federal Ministry of Family Affairs, Senior Citizens, Women and Youth
→ **bmfsfj.de**

Federal Ministry of Health
→ **bundesgesundheitsministerium.de**

Federal Ministry of Transport and Digital Infrastructure
→ **bmvi.de**

Federal Ministry for the Environment, Nature Conservation and Nuclear Safety
→ **bmu.de**

Federal Ministry of Education and Research
→ **bmbf.de**

Federal Ministry for Economic Cooperation and Development
→ **bmz.de**

Federal Presidents & Federal Chancellors

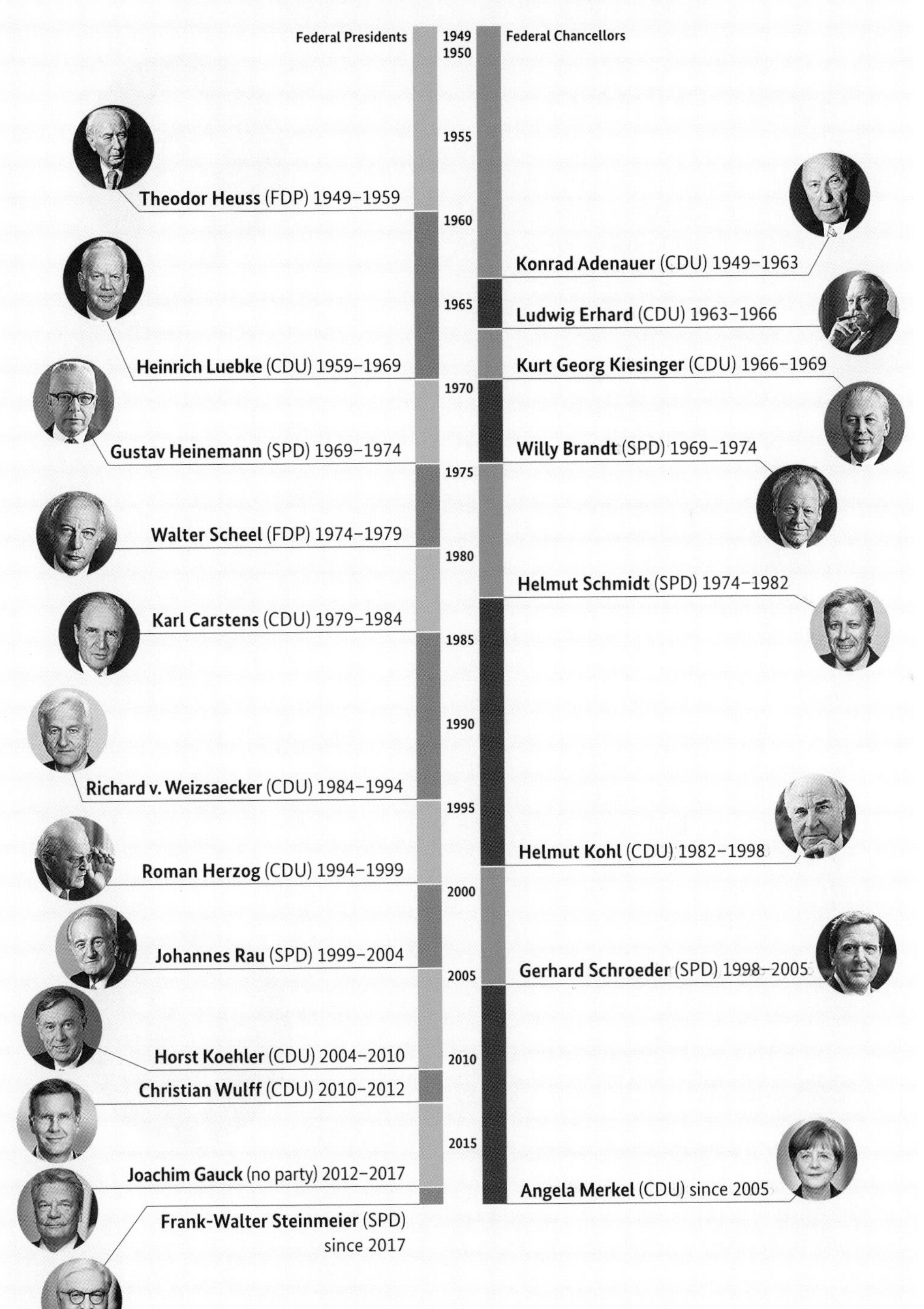

FAMOUS GERMANS

Celebrated classics, courageous visionaries, astute thinkers: Germany's history is rich in people who achieved extraordinary things. Many of them are famous far beyond the country's borders. The Goethe-Institut has been indirectly spreading the name of the best-known of all Germans, Johann Wolfgang von Goethe, throughout the world since 1951. Wagner fans from all over the world congregate every year at the Bayreuth Festival to pay homage to "Der Ring des Nibelungen". Names such as Humboldt and Einstein, Röntgen and Planck, Benz and Otto established Germany's reputation as a country of researchers and engineers. They were followed by Stefan Hell, Nobel Prize Laureate for Chemistry, and astronaut Alexander Gerst.

In earlier days, women faced difficulties leading similarly high-profile lives. Yet there are nonetheless many famous women, such as Clara Schumann, Maria Sibylla Merian, Paula Modersohn-Becker, Rosa Luxemburg, Anna Seghers, Sophie Scholl, and the great choreograph Pina Bausch. Today, writer and poet Herta Müller and researcher Christiane Nüsslein-Volhard are just two examples of women who have achieved outstanding work. All these women are regarded as role models for a modern society which enables men and women alike to participate and enjoy equal opportunities – even though this still requires a concerted effort. ■

Johann Wolfgang von Goethe

Poet, playwright, scholar: Johann Wolfgang von Goethe (1749–1832) is regarded as an all-round genius and the classic in German literature.

Friedrich von Schiller

A fighter for freedom: Friedrich von Schiller (1759–1805) is regarded as one of the world's great playwrights ("The Robbers", "Mary Stuart", "Don Carlos") and as an important essayist.

Johann Sebastian Bach

Virtuoso of Baroque church music: Johann Sebastian Bach (1685–1750) perfected the strict "art of the fugue" and composed more than 200 cantatas and oratorios.

Marlene Dietrich

The film diva: Marlene Dietrich (1901–1992) was one of only a few German actresses to become an icon ("The Blue Angel"). Born in Berlin, she took US citizenship in 1939.

Ludwig van Beethoven

Pioneer of Romanticism: Ludwig van Beethoven (1770–1827), focussing clearly on form, brought a completely new measure of personal expression and sensitivity to bear in music ("9th Symphony").

Thomas Mann

A master of the novel and novella: Thomas Mann (1875–1955) is one of the most important authors of 20th-century world literature. In 1929 he was awarded the Nobel Prize in Literature for his family saga "Buddenbrooks".

Albrecht Dürer

German Renaissance artist: Albrecht Dürer (1471–1528) from Nuremberg is one of the most important and versatile figures in the history of art. He revolutionised woodcarving and copperplate engraving techniques.

Wilhelm Conrad Röntgen

Discoverer of X-rays: Wilhelm Conrad Röntgen (1845–1923) discovered X-rays in 1895 in Würzburg. In 1901 he was awarded the Nobel Prize in Physics. Since then more than 80 leading German scientists have received a Nobel Prize.

Willy Brandt

Politician and cosmopolitan: Willy Brandt (1913–1992) as Federal Chancellor from 1969–1974 initiated a policy of detente; like no other he embodied the democratic and social changes of the time – in 1971 he received the Nobel Peace Prize.

THE STATE & POLITICS

New Tasks • Federal State • Active Politics • Broad Participation • Political Berlin • Vibrant Culture of Remembrance

INSIGHT

NEW TASKS

Germany is a value-based, democratic, economically successful, and cosmopolitan country. The political landscape is diverse. Following the elections for the 19th German Bundestag (2017) initially the CDU/CSU, which emerged from the elections as the largest party, explored the option of a coalition government with the FDP and Alliance 90/The Greens. The talks failed. Subsequently the CDU/CSU and SPD formed a Grand Coalition in March 2018 after tough coalition talks and an SPD members' vote. The previous legislative period had already seen such an alliance of the two strongest forces in the German party system. Of the 709 Members of Parliament, the coalition partners account for 399 seats (CDU/CSU 246, SPD 153). The opposition consists of the AfD (92 seats), FDP (80), The Left party (69) and Alliance 90/The Greens (67), plus two independent MPs. The right-wing populist Alternative für Deutschland (Alternative for Germany, AfD) is represented in the Bundestag for the first time. Federal Chancellor Dr. Angela Merkel (CDU) has been head of government since 2005 and is now in her fourth term. She is the first woman in the history of the Federal Republic of Germany to hold this office. Deputy Chancellor Olaf Scholz (Federal Minister of Finance) and Heiko Maas (Federal Foreign Minister) are important representatives of the SPD in the Cabinet. The Cabinet is made up of 14 ministers and the Head of the Federal Chancellery. The Coalition Agreement entitled "A New Awakening for Europe, a New Dynamic for Germany, a New Cohesion for Our Country" serves as the basis of the government parties' joint work.

In 2018, the German economy will enter its ninth year of consecutive growth, employment is at a record high, and government revenue and national insurance contributions have ▸

VIDEO AR APP

The State & Politics: the video on the topic → **tued.net/en/vid1**

The Reichstag Building in Berlin has been the seat of the German Bundestag since 1999. Sir Norman Foster designed the glass dome

risen. New debt assumed by central government has been reduced to zero. The Energy Transition is being driven forward – renewable energies are on the way to becoming the decisive technology for generating electricity.

Together, the people in Germany have made the gradual fusion of east and west Germany, a major issue since Reunification in 1990, into a success story. The "Solidarity Pact II", for which 156.5 billion euros are set aside, will remain in force until 2019. All tax-paying citizens in the east and west continue to play a joint role in the "Aufbau Ost" project to redevelop the east through the "solidarity surcharge", a supplementary contribution which today stands at 5.5 percent of personal income tax.

That said, new tasks await. As in other industrialised countries, demographic change is regarded as a challenge. The topics of immigration and integration are also high on the agenda. The result of the Bundestag elections is an expression of the uncertainty and dissatisfaction felt by many people, and as such the Federal Government aims to, as stated in the Coalition Agreement, "safeguard that which is good, but at the same time demonstrate the courage to engage in political debate and bring about renewal and change". ■

INTERNET

The German Bundestag
Elections, Members of Parliament, parliamentary groups
→ **bundestag.de**

The Bundesrat
Composition, duties, sessions
→ **bundesrat.de**

The Federal President
State visits, appointments, duties
→ **bundespraesident.de**

Chaired by Federal Chancellor Merkel, the federal cabinet meets every Wednesday at 9.30 a.m. in the Federal Chancellery

COMPACT

PLAYERS & ORGANISATIONS

Political parties

Germany is a party-based democracy. Seven parties are represented in the 19th German Bundestag – CDU, CSU, SPD, AfD, FDP, The Left party, and Alliance 90/The Greens. There are also around 25 small parties, whose influence is limited on account of the five-percent hurdle. Some of them are represented, however, in various federal state parliaments. The Social Democratic Party of Germany (SPD) is the party with the most members (463,700). The Christian Democratic Union (CDU) has around 427,000 members, its sister party the Christian Social Union (CSU) in Bavaria 141,000 (2017).

→ bundeswahlleiter.de

Trade unions

The German Trade Union Confederation (DGB) embraces eight individual trade unions and has 6 million members. With 2.3 million members IG Metall, the metal workers' union, which among other things represents workers in the automotive sector, is the single largest union. The trade unions' ideas have weight and influence in political debates.

→ dgb.de

Industrial federations

As industry's umbrella organisation, the Federation of German Industries (BDI) unites 35 sector federations and speaks on behalf of around 100,000 companies.

→ bdi.de

Social movements

Since the 1970s many people in Germany have been actively involved in environmental groups, citizens' movements, and non-government organisations. With over half a million members, Friends of the Earth Germany (BUND) is the largest environmental association.

→ bund.net

Public opinion research

Numerous opinion research institutes regularly conduct research into the political climate in Germany. Institutes such as infratest dimap, Allensbach, Forsa, Emnid, and Forschungsgruppe Wahlen have a particularly strong presence in the run-up to elections, but also with up-to-date weekly barometers that indicate the general mood.

DIGITAL PLUS

More information about all the topics in the chapter – annotated link lists, articles, documents; plus more in-depth information about terms such as Bundesrat, Federal Government, federal state, Bundestag, Federal Constitutional Court, Basic Law, electoral system.

→ tued.net/en/dig1

TOPIC
FEDERAL STATE

Germany is a parliamentary and federal democracy. The German Bundestag, the constitutional body most present in the public eye, is directly elected by citizens eligible to vote every four years. The most important tasks of the Bundestag are legislation and to oversee the government's work. The Bundestag elects the Federal Chancellor for the legislative period by secret ballot. Within the Federal Government the Chancellor has the authority to lay down guidelines, in other words determines binding broad policy lines. The Federal Chancellor appoints the federal ministers, and from among them a Deputy Chancellor. In actual fact, however, it is the parties that make up the government that decide which persons will head the ministries they were allocated in the coalition negotiations. If a coalition collapses, the Chancellor can also fall prior to the end of the electoral term, as the Federal Government has the right to vote the head of government out of office at any time. In such cases parliament must, however, name a successor at the same time in what is known as a "constructive vote of no confidence". This means that there can be no period of time without an elected government in office.

Coalition governments are the rule in Germany

The system of personalised proportional representation is decisive with regard to the character of the parliament. This way, smaller parties are also represented in the Bundestag in proportion to their election results. For this reason, with one exception, the Federal Government has always been formed through an alliance of several parties that had competed against each other in the election; since the first Bundestag election in 1949 there have been 24 coalition governments. To avoid fragmentation in parliament and make forming a government easier, parties must poll at least five per cent of the votes cast (or three direct mandates) in order to be represented in the Bundestag (this rule is known as the five percent hurdle).

LIST

- Largest federal state: **North Rhine-Westphalia (17.9 million inhabitants)**
- Highest individual federal ministry budget: **Labour and Social Affairs (137.6 billion euros)**
- Largest Bundestag committee: **Economic Affairs and Energy (49 members)**
- Highest turnout: **1972 election to the Bundestag (91.1 percent)**
- Largest parl. party: **CDU/CSU (246 MPs)**

On the roof of the Reichstag in Berlin: around 8,000 people visit the parliamentary building every day

Germany's federal character is revealed in the large level of independence the 16 federal states enjoy, in particular with regard to the police, disaster control, the law, and culture. For historical reasons the cities of Berlin, Hamburg, and Bremen are also federal states. The close links between the federal states and central government is unique, resulting in the state governments having numerous opportunities to play an active role in central government policy. This occurs primarily through the Bundesrat, the upper house, which is made up of members of the federal state governments and is likewise in Berlin. Densely populated federal states have greater representation in the Bundesrat than smaller ones. By being coalition partners in federal state governments, parties that at federal level are in opposition, or not even represented in the Bundestag, can thus potentially exert an influence on politics at federal level, as numerous federal acts and ▸

▸ decrees require the approval of the Bundesrat. Since 2011 and 2014 the two smallest parties represented in the Bundestag, Alliance 90/The Greens and The Left party, have provided the Prime Minister in one federal state each (Baden-Wurttemberg and Thuringia respectively).

Because there is no uniform election date for the federal state parliaments and the legislature periods vary, parallel to the legislative term in the Bundestag the balance of power in the Bundesrat can change several times. With the current constellation of the chamber of federal states, the Federal Government has no safe majority in the Bundesrat. There are no longer any distinct blocks demonstrating uniform voting behaviour, as there is more diversity with regard to coalitions in the 16 federal states than ever before in the Federal Republic.

Only in Bavaria can a single party, the CSU, rule without a coalition partner. Otherwise, in spring 2018, in addition to four state governments made up of the CDU and SPD parties there were two combinations of SPD and Greens, two of CDU and Greens, one of SPD and The Left party, two coalitions of The Left party, SPD, and Greens and one coalition each of CDU and FDP; of CDU, Greens, and FDP; of SPD, FDP, and Greens; and of SPD, CDU, and Greens.

The Federal President is the most senior political person in the country

In terms of protocol the Federal President holds the highest office. He is elected not by the people, but by a Federal Assembly convened specially for the purpose. Half of it is made up of the members of the Bundestag, the other half of members elected by the federal state parliaments in relation to the distribution of seats there. The Federal President holds office for five years and may be re-elected once. Dr. Frank-Walter Steinmeier has been Federal President since 2017. As an SPD politician he served as Federal Foreign Minister from 2005 until 2009 and from 2013 until 2017. Steinmeier is the 12th Federal President since 1949. Although the Federal President's duties are

MILESTONES

1949

On 23 May the Parliamentary Council, which is made up of representatives of the states in the Western Occupation Zones, rresolves the Basic Law in Bonn. The first Bundestag is elected on 14 August.

1953

On 17 June 1953 around one million people take to the streets in East Berlin and East Germany in protest at the political and economic conditions. The uprising is quashed by a massive military operation.

1961

In Berlin, the East German leadership seals off the crossings from east to west: with a wall and barbed wire. Anyone henceforth seen trying to escape is shot. The unity of Germany as a state seems unattainable for the foreseeable future.

primarily representational in nature, he can refuse to put his signature to legislation if he has doubts about it complying with the constitution. Previous incumbents have exerted the greatest influence through public speeches, which receive great attention. The Federal Presidents refrain from becoming involved in party politics, but do tackle current issues and from time to time urge the government, parliament, and the population to take action. During the formation of a government following the 2017 Bundestag elections, which, for Germany, was an unusually protracted process, it was important to Steinmeier to avoid fresh elections. Without his intervention, it is unlikely the SPD would have entered into a Grand Coalition at this point in time.

GLOBAL

Office for Democratic Institutions and Human Rights, Elections of the Federal Parliament (Bundestag) At the invitation of Germany, the Organization for Security and Co-operation in Europe (OSCE) observed the election of the Bundestag on 24 September 2017. In their report, the OSCE experts certified that Germany conducted a fair election which was not influenced by manipulations, such as by hackers.

→ **osce.org**

OSCE

BUNDESREPUBLIK DEUTSCHLAND

WAHLEN ZUM DEUTSCHEN BUNDESTAG

Office for Democratic Institutions and Human Rights

OSCE ODIHR

The Federal Constitutional Court in Karlsruhe: guardian of the Basic Law

The Federal Constitutional Court in Karlsruhe, which the population holds in very high esteem, exerts great influence. It is regarded as "the guardian of the Basic Law" and through its important decisions provides a binding interpretation of the constitutional text. In two panels it passes judgement on disputes between constitutional bodies about areas of jurisdiction, and can declare laws to be incompatible with the Basic Law. Any citizen can appeal to the Constitutional Court if he is of the opinion that a law violates his basic rights. ■

1969
Willy Brandt is the first Chancellor not to be a member of the CDU party. The Ostpolitik of the coalition government made up of the SPD and FDP creates a framework for the reconciliation of Germany with its eastern neighbours.

1989-90
In East Germany, peaceful protests lead to the regime being toppled. On 9 November the border with the West is opened. After the first free elections on 18 March, East Germany accedes to the Federal Republic on 3 October 1990.

1999
The Bundestag and the Federal Government are relocated to Berlin. The parliamentary buildings stand on both sides of the former course taken by the Wall. Bonn remains the seat of some ministries and federal authorities.

TOPIC
ACTIVE POLITICS

"A New Beginning for Europe. New dynamism for Germany. New cohesion for our country" is the title the Grand Coalition chose for its government programme until 2021. It seeks to champion strengthening the European Union as a guarantor for peace, security and prosperity. With its objective of a balanced budget, which has been achieved since 2014, the Federal Government considers itself responsible for monetary stability, and wishes to be a role model for its partners in the Eurozone. At the same time, it has indicated a willingness to make a larger contribution to the EU budget. Together with France, the Federal Government wants to strengthen and reform the Eurozone to enable the euro to better withstand global crises.

For Germany, it wants to ensure that everyone benefits from the good economic situation. This should create greater social justice and reinforce people's trust in the ability of politics to act effectively.

The results of the 2017 general elections spelled strong losses for the major parties that had formed the last government. By contrast, the right-wing populaist AfD made large gains and entered the Bundestag as the largest opposition party. Despite the ongoing favourable economic conditions, many people are concerned about the future. Not least this led the Federal Government to conclude that it needed to foster social cohesion in the country and overcome divisions. It has thus set out specifically to strengthen families, improve provisions for old age and unemployment, and promote education, innovations, and digitisation. One key element is to more carefully control immigration and improve the integration of migrants. The Basic Law assures politically persecuted persons a basic right to asylum. Germany will continue to help people in distress who have a right to asylum. At the same time, the Federal Government is intensifying its efforts to have people who have no prospect of being able to reside in Germany leave the country again. The Federal Government hopes that the reform of the Common European Asylum System will be concluded by 2018.

\# NUMBER

0 euros

was what Germany's federal budget deficit came to in 2017. While expenditure totalled 325.4 billion euros, revenue amounted to 330.4 billion euros. For the fourth year in succession, in 2017 central government assumed no new debt. This was thanks above all to higher tax revenues generated by the robust economy.

→ **bundeshaushalt-info.de**

The Bundestag in Berlin is the political stage. There are 709 members of the 19th German Bundestag

Following on from successes

In the prior legislative period, the Bundestag for the first time resolved a minimum wage for all sectors. In 2018, it was EUR 8.84 per hour of work and will continue to be reviewed regularly. A quota for women in large stock corporations was introduced in 2016. As of the end of 2017 companies have been meeting the requirement that at least 30 percent of the members of a supervisory board must be women. At the end of 2017, women accounted for 25 percent of the supervisory board members of Germany's 200 largest corporations. Advancing the Energy Transition, through which Germany has already increased its share of regenerative energies significantly, as well as the expansion of the digital infrastructure are further focal points. ■

TOPIC

BROAD PARTICIPATION

The political parties are granted a major and privileged place in the political system of the Federal Republic of Germany. Article 21 of the Basic Law states that "Political parties shall participate in the formation of the political will of the people." This goes hand in hand with an obligation to uphold inner-party democracy: The chairperson, committees, and candidates must all be elected by secret ballot of grass roots delegates at party conferences. In order to strengthen this inner-party democracy, in the case of important decisions parties have in recent times polled their members directly. The SPD members' vote on the Coalition Agreement in 2018 was pivotal to the forming of a joint Federal Government with the CDU/CSU. At heart the parties are still expressions of specific strata of society, but at the same time they are losing coherence in this regard. CDU/CSU and SPD together have around one million party members – in relation to the 61.5 million eligible voters that is a share of 1.7 percent. There is also a downward trend in election turnout. Whereas in the 1970s and 1980s elections continually saw high and extremely high turnouts, (91.1 percent in 1972), in 2013 and 2017 the elections to the Bundestag only saw turnouts of 71.5 and 76.2 percent respectively.

Young people often find being involved in local citizens' groups and non-government organisations more appealing. Social media are also becoming increasingly important as platforms for a specific type of political articulation and action. Citizens also participate directly in political issues through democratic procedures such as referendums. Over the past few years, there have been more opportunities for direct democracy at both federal state and municipal level, and citizens have made great use of these. ■

DIAGRAM

The voice of the people

In Germany voting is on the basis of slightly modified personalised proportional representation. Every person eligible to vote has two votes. The first is for a party's candidate in the constituency, the second for a state list of candidates put up by a particular party. The second votes are the basis of the number of seats in the Bundestag.

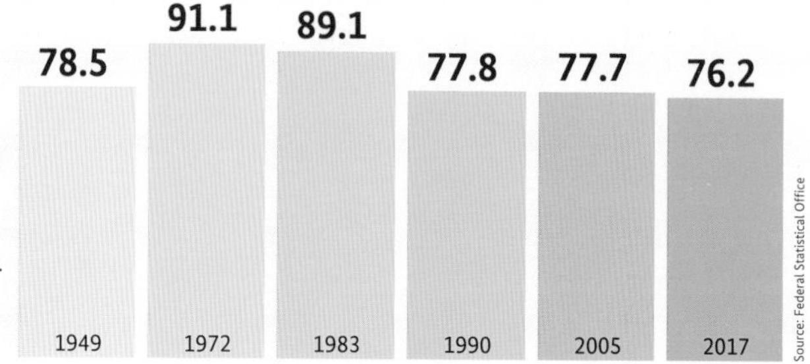

The instruments of direct democracy, such as referendums, come into play more frequently at the municipal level

Age structure of those entitled to vote

3.6 %	18–21 years
11.8 %	21–30 years
13.9 %	30–40 years
14.7 %	40–50 years
20 %	50–60 years
15.4 %	60–70 years
20.7 %	70 and older

Turnout for referendums

Referendum	Turnout
Baden-Wurttemberg (2011)	48.3 %
Berlin (2014)	46.1 %
Hamburg (2010)	39.3 %
Bavaria (2010)	37.7 %

Sources: Federal Statistical Office, returning officers, referendums

PANORAMA

POLITICAL BERLIN

❶ Bellevue Palace
Built in the late 18th century, Bellevue Palace has been the official residence of Germany's Federal President since 1994. It is located on the edge of Berlin's Tiergarten district.

❷ Federal Chancellery
The new Federal Chancellery went into service in 2001. The outside of the post-Modernist building is predominantly glazed. "Berlin", a steel sculpture by Basque artist Eduardo Chillida, is situated in the "Ehrenhof" (courtyard of honour).

709
MPs make up the 19th German Bundestag

31 %
of MPs in the Bundestag are women

61,500,000
Germans are eligible to vote in elections to the Bundestag

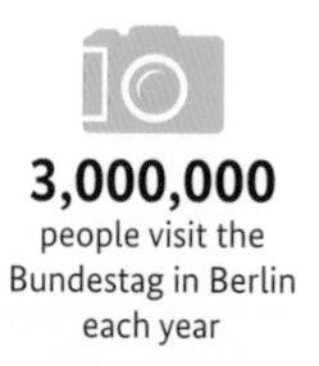

3,000,000
people visit the Bundestag in Berlin each year

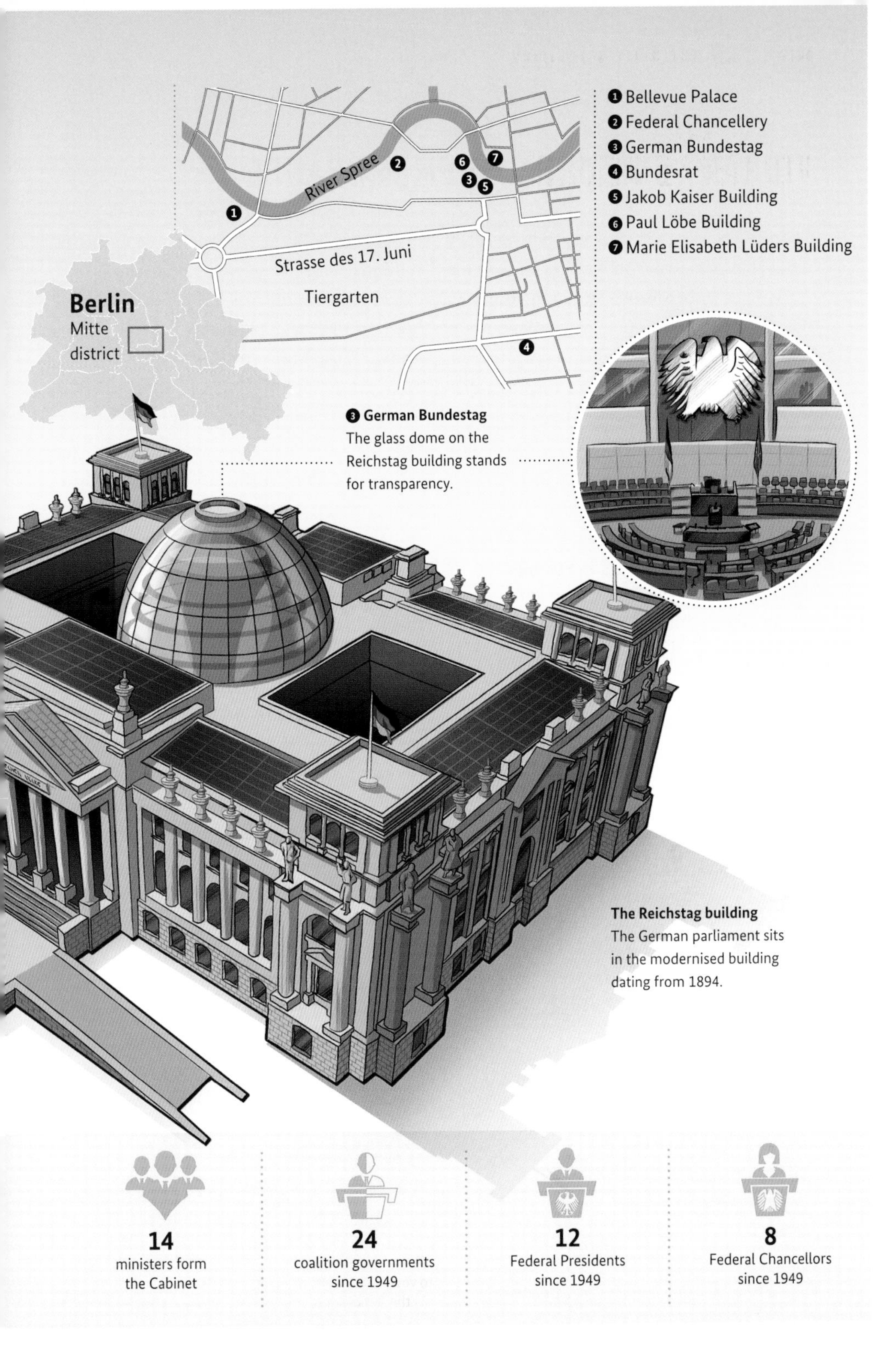

River Spree
Strasse des 17. Juni
Tiergarten
Berlin
Mitte district
1 Bellevue Palace
2 Federal Chancellery
3 German Bundestag
4 Bundesrat
5 Jakob Kaiser Building
6 Paul Löbe Building
7 Marie Elisabeth Lüders Building
3 German Bundestag
The glass dome on the Reichstag building stands for transparency.
The Reichstag building
The German parliament sits in the modernised building dating from 1894.
14
ministers form the Cabinet
24
coalition governments since 1949
12
Federal Presidents since 1949
8
Federal Chancellors since 1949

TOPIC

VIBRANT CULTURE OF REMEMBRANCE

Addressing war and tyranny, ideologically motivated crimes and political injustice in the 20th century, not to mention commemorating the victims of persecution, play an important role in the culture of remembrance in the Federal Republic of Germany. Preserving eyewitness reports by persons who actually experienced the events is the key element in a culture of remembrance destined to make certain that coming generations are conscious of the crimes committed by the Nazis. The numerous memorials to the various groups of victims all over Germany are also part of this vibrant culture of remembrance. In central Berlin, for example, the Memorial to the Murdered Jews of Europe is a memorial to the six million Jewish victims of the Holocaust.

INFO

"Stolpersteine"

In many German and European cities, "Stolpersteine" (stumbling stones) placed in the ground remind passers-by that Jewish citizens who were persecuted, murdered, deported, or driven away by the Nazis, once lived or worked in the buildings outside which the stones are placed. The approximately 10 by 10-centimetre cube-shaped concrete blocks have a brass top with an inscription in memory of the victim bearing his or her name and biographical data.

→ stolpersteine.eu

Memorials to war, resistance and dictatorship

In November 2018 Germany commemorates the end of the First World War a century ago; 2019 is the 100th anniversary of the inaugural meeting of the Weimar Republic's National Assembly, the first German democracy. In the major anniversary years 2014 and 2015 too, marking the 100th anniversary of the beginning of the First World War and the 25th anniversary of the fall of the Berlin Wall, the overwhelming sentiment in the memorial services was one of gratitude. Gratitude for the Allies' anti-Hitler coalition for liberating Germany in 1945, and for the opportunity to re-build the country and for its reunification in 1990. There was also gratitude to those who, as surviving victims of the Holocaust, bore witness to the crimes – and reached out their hand to a democratic Germany after the Second World War.

Memories of the communist dictatorship during the Soviet Occupation Zone (1945–1949) and the days of East Germany (1949–1990) are also being kept alive for those generations that never experienced the division of Germany and the East German system. The Federal Commissioner for the Records of the State Security Service of the Former

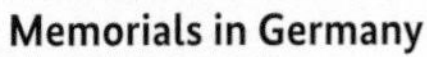

MAP

Memorials in Germany

German Democratic Republic, the institution where files are still being examined, sorted, and made accessible to those affected and academics, plays a major role in this. A permanent exhibition in the former headquarters of the State Security Service (Stasi) of the German Democratic Republic (GDR) in Berlin's Hohenschönhausen district provides an insight into the means and methods the Stasi used to spy on, control, and intimidate the population.

In the "Bendlerblock" in the Mitte district of Berlin the German Resistance Memorial Centre is devoted to the resistance to the Nazi dictatorship. It is located on the historical site of the failed coup attempted by the group headed by Count Stauffenberg on 20 July 1944. The Memorial Centre impressively documents how, between 1933 and 1945, individuals and groups took action against the dictatorship of the Third Reich and made use of what freedom of action they had. ■

FOREIGN POLICY

Civil Policy-Shaping Power • Committed to Peace and Security • Advocate of European Integration • Protection of Human Rights • Open Network Partner • Sustainable Development

INSIGHT

CIVIL POLICY-SHAPING POWER

On the international stage, Germany enjoys a very broad network of close contacts. It maintains diplomatic relations with almost 200 countries and is a member of all the important multilateral organisations and informal international coordination groups such as the "Group of Seven" (G7) and the "Group of Twenty" (G20). Heiko Maas (SPD) has been Federal Foreign Minister since 2018. The Federal Foreign Office, which is based in Berlin, has around 11,652 staff members. In total, Germany maintains 227 missions abroad.

The primary objective of German foreign policy is to ensure peace and security in the world. The basic premises on which this rests include the nation's full integration into the structures of multilateral cooperation. In concrete terms this means: close partnership with France in the European Union (EU), firm roots in the community of values shaped by the transatlantic alliance with the USA, support of the right of Israel to exist, active and committed involvement in the United Nations (UN) and the Council of Europe, as well as the strengthening of the European security structure through the OSCE.

Together with its partners, Germany promotes peace, security, democracy, and human rights all over the world. Alongside crisis prevention, disarmament, and arms control, the broad notion of security promulgated by Germany embraces sustainable economic, ecological, and social aspects. These include a globalisation that offers opportunities for everyone, cross-border environmental and climate protection, dialogue between cultures, and openness towards guests and immigrants.

▶

VIDEO AR APP

Foreign policy: the video on the topic
→ **tued.net/en/vid2**

German foreign policy is firmly embedded in multilateral cooperation

▸ **Since the end** of the East-West conflict, new opportunities and challenges have emerged for German foreign policy. On the basis of its multilateral relations, Germany has accepted the increased responsibility it has been accorded since reunification in 1990. Through its many efforts, Germany nowadays plays a role in the political resolution of conflicts, the maintenance of peacekeeping structures, and crisis prevention as part of UN-mandated peace missions. To further support the UN in crisis prevention, Germany has trebled its contribution in this area, as Foreign Minister Maas stated in a speech to the UN in spring 2018.

Security requires more than military defence, and Germany is also increasing its efforts in humanitarian assistance and in foreign cultural policy. Germany has underscored its commitment by its successful candidacy for a non-permanent seat on the UN Security Council in 2019-20.

In the age of globalisation and digitisation and against the backdrop of a fast-changing world, alongside classical foreign policy new fields are increasingly on the agenda, including, for example, "malign cyberoperations" or attempts via propaganda to influence public opinion. ■

→ INTERNET

Federal Foreign Office
Appointments, people, issues, contacts
→ **diplo.de**

European Union
Portal of the community of states with information in 24 languages
→ **europa.eu**

OSCE
Permanent mission of the Federal Republic of Germany to the OSCE
→ **osze.diplo.de**

Federal Foreign Minister Maas and EU High Representative for Foreign Affairs and Security Policy Federica Mogherini (right)

COMPACT

PLAYERS & ORGANISATIONS

Diplomatic missions
Germany maintains diplomatic relations with 195 countries and has a global presence with 227 missions, 153 of them embassies. Germany has permanent representatives at 12 international organisations.
→ diplo.de

Multilateral organisations
Germany assumes responsibility in multilateral organisations such as the United Nations (UN), the European Union (EU), the North Atlantic Alliance (NATO), the Organization for Security and Co-operation in Europe (OSCE), the European Council, the Organisation for Economic Co-Operation and Development (OECD), the World Trade Organization (WTO), and the International Monetary Fund (IMF).

German Armed Forces
Following an internal reform the German Armed Forces now has around 180,000 active soldiers, of which 21,000 are women. In 2018, a total of 3,700 members of the German Armed Forces were deployed to missions in 14 different crisis areas.
→ bundeswehr.de

Experts in conflict prevention
The Centre for International Peace Operations trains civilian specialists for missions in crisis regions and provides experts.
→ zif-berlin.org

Foreign policy think tanks
Important foreign and security policy research institutes include the German Council on Foreign Relations (DGAP), the German Institute of Global and Area Studies (GIGA), the Peace Research Institute Frankfurt (PRIF), the Institute for Peace Research and Security Policy (IFSH), and German Institute for International and Security Affairs (SWP).

Political foundations
The foundations closely associated with the German political parties CDU, CSU, SPD, The Left party, Alliance 90/The Greens, and FDP have offices worldwide. With federal funds, they promote dialogue and development in partner countries.

DIGITAL PLUS

More information about all the topics in the chapter – annotated link lists, articles, documents, speeches; plus more in-depth information about the European Union as well as short portraits of the multilateral organisations.
→ tued.net/en/dig2

TOPIC

COMMITTED TO PEACE AND SECURITY

Diplomacy, crisis prevention, and peaceful conflict resolution are the primary German foreign policy instruments: Deploying civil servants, judges, public prosecutors, police officers, reconstruction experts, and other civil officers is one strand of Germany's comprehensive security policy, as is the German Armed Forces' participation in multinational peacekeeping missions. The defining feature of German foreign policy, close multilateral involvement, applies in particular to the deployment of military means. Crisis management missions by the German Armed Forces always take place within the framework of the systems of collective security or defence run by international organisations such as the United Nations (UN), the European Union (EU) or the North Atlantic Treaty Organization (NATO). The deployment of German Armed Forces abroad is embedded in a broader political approach with civilian elements such as political development-policy or socio-economic measures. The Federal Government has developed guidelines for its international commitment in the context of crises. Each deployment of armed forces is subject to parliamentary mandate and control. It requires approval by the majority of the members of the Bundestag. The German Armed Forces are therefore also termed a parliamentary army.

LIST

- Largest German foreign mission: **Moscow embassy, about 300 staff**
- Largest parliamentary group in the German Bundestag: **Parliamentary Group USA, 80 members of parliament**
- Largest EU body in Germany: **European Central Bank (ECB) in Frankfurt am Main, 3,380 staff members**
- UN organisations in Germany: **in total 30, 19 of them in Bonn**

Germany has been a political and military member of NATO ever since the German Armed Forces were set up in 1955. This firm anchoring in NATO is part of German foreign policy's DNA. Germany is the second largest provider of troops to NATO and contributes substantially to NATO-led missions, such as the Resolute Support Mission (RSM) in Afghanistan or the KFOR in Kosovo. Since 1992, some 40 foreign missions have been carried out. In spring 2018, the German Armed Forces had deployed about 3,500 soldiers on 14 missions. As a result of the Ukraine crisis, NATO has focussed more strongly on the core task of Alliance defence and resolved a number of adaptation and safeguarding measures. Germany plays a major role here: In 2015, together with the

Netherlands and Norway, the country helped set up the new, very high readiness joint task force (VJTF) which improves the Alliance's response capabilities. In 2019 the German Armed Forces will again, on a rotation basis, as a Framework Nation play a leading role in VJTF. Moreover, Germany is contributing to policing the Baltic states' air space and since 2017 as a Framework Nation has contributed in Lithuania to NATO's enhanced forward presence in the Baltic states and Poland.

Reliable and respected UN member

Since being accepted into the UN in 1973, the Federal Republic of Germany has been an active, reliable, and respected member of the organisation. In 2018 Germany was elected a non-permanent member of the UN Security Council for the sixth time. Each year, Germany contributes some 161 million US dollars to the regular UN budget, and about 466 million dollars to the budget for UN peacekeeping missions, in each case 6.4 percent of the total UN budget. In 2017-8 Germany was thus the fourth largest contributor. In the 2013-7 period, Germany quadrupled its payments to the United Nations High Commission for Refugees (UNHCR). With 387 million euros a year, Germany is the second-largest donor after the USA. In spring 2018 Germany took part in five UN peacekeeping missions, among others in Mali and in Lebanon. Of the Western industrialised nations, Germany provides the most troops for UN peacekeeping missions. The UN has a strong presence in Germany, in particular at the UN Campus in Bonn, where 19 of a total of 30 UN agencies in Germany are based.

To optimise support for peacekeeping missions by international organisations, Germany is further professionalising the training and posting of civilian crisis workers. Founded in 2002, the ZIF Centre for International Peace Missions has a pool of 1,500 experts on standby, with plans for further expansion. ZIF selects civilian experts, holds courses preparing them for postings as observers or arbiters in crisis zones and post-conflict countries, and evaluates their experiences. In collaboration with the Federal Foreign Office, the ZIF has meanwhile posted about 3,000 voluntary short and long-term election observers on missions and realised projects in 65 countries.

As another key pillar of peace and security in Europe, Germany supports the Organization for Security and Co-operation in Europe (OSCE), which has its origins in 1995 in the Conference on Security and Co-operation in Europe (CSCE). The baseline document for the OSCE is the Helsinki Final Act signed in 1975, agreeing amongst other things the inviolability of borders and the peaceful solution of conflicts as the principles of a European security order.

The OSCE as central forum for peace and security in Europe

Today, the organisation has 57 participating states from Europe, North America, and Central Asia, and it is thus the world's largest re- ▸

The German Armed Forces are involved in numerous missions abroad, e.g. the European Training Mission in Mali (EUTM)

▸ gional organisation for collective security. The OSCE maintains permanent missions in many countries to prevent conflicts and promote democratisation, and, something Germany also supports, regularly sends election observers to participating states. During the Ukraine crisis, the OSCE's significance as a key tool for crisis management and a forum for dialogue and confidence building was once again manifest. The OSCE supports the efforts to solve the conflict in east Ukraine, amongst other things by moderating political negotiations and by a special monitoring mission, whereby some 650 civilian monitors in the area in conflict supervise compliance with the Minsk Agreement and try to verify the withdrawal of troops and weapons. Under the German chairmanship, the OSCE in 2016 resurrected past negotiation formats for other flashpoints (Transniestria, Nagorno-Karabakh). To restore trust and strengthen the OSCE as a platform for dialogue on security policy, the OSCE Ministerial Council in Hamburg at the end of 2016 decided to mandate a structured dialogue on security-policy challenges in Europe and their impact on armaments control policies ("From Lisbon to Hamburg").

Championing disarmament and arms controls

Germany makes an important contribution to global security with its disarmament, arms control, and non-proliferation activities. Germany's goal is a world without nuclear weapons. For example, Germany seeks the swift implementation of the Nuclear Test Ban Treaty. Together with the five permanent members of the UN Security Council and the European Union, Germany actively helped ensure that in July 2015 the Vienna Nuclear

Agreement with Iran on the Iranian nuclear programme was concluded. Moreover, Germany advocates the universal validity and enforcement of the relevant international agreements and treaties, e.g. the Chemical Weapons Convention, which sets out the norm of the non-deployment of chemical weapons.

Germany has also taken a clear position on arms control policy issues relating to new technologies, such as autonomous weapons systems. The Federal Government rejects fully autonomous weapons systems that undermine a final decision being subject to human control and seeks to ensure a global ban on such weapons. One goal of German foreign policy is the global realisation of the "Ottawa Convention", the central treaty for banning anti-personnel mines.

In 2017 Germany contributed about 75.7 million euros for projects to clear mines and care for the victims of mines, making it one of the largest donors in this area. German policies also focus on the destruction of surplus weapons and ammunition and the safe storage of dangerous substances.

Conventional disarmament controls and confidence and security-building measures are very important within the OSCE area. Germany advocates modernising and adapting these controls to current challenges and in 2016 initiated the relaunch of conventional armaments controls in Europe. The "Structured Dialogue" inaugurated at the Hamburg OSCE Ministerial Council Meeting at the end of 2016 emerged in 2017 under the German chairmanship as a crucial forum for the security architecture in the OSCE framework. It is designed to help discuss perceptions of threats, reanimate security cooperation and strengthen conventional arms controls. ■

GLOBAL

Armed Conflict Survey 2017 According to the International Institute for Strategic Studies (IISS) in London, in 2016 the number of war victims dipped. In 36 armed conflicts, in 2016 about 157,000 people lost their lives, roughly 10,000 less than in 2015. The war in Syria was the world's most violent conflict. 90 percent of Syrian refugees settled in neighbouring countries. At the end of 2016, a total of 65.6 million people were refugees.

→ **iiss.org**

TOPIC

ADVOCATE OF EUROPEAN INTEGRATION

No country in Europe has more neighbours than Germany. It shares its border with nine countries, eight of which are European Union (EU) member states. For Germany, European integration, one of the most impressive political success stories, lays the foundations for peace, security, and prosperity. Advancing and strengthening this, particularly in view of complex and in many cases crisis-ridden conditions, remains the main task of German foreign policy. Begun in the early 1950s, the historical project that today is the EU nowadays has over half a billion citizens in 28 member states. German European policy emerged as a driving force in all stages of European unification, and actively helped shape the process of European cohesion following the end of the East-West conflict. This European integration created the world's largest common market, characterised by the four fundamental freedoms formulated in the 1957 Treaty of Rome: the free movement of goods between the EU member states, the freedom of movement of persons, the freedom to provide services within the EU, and the free flow of capital.

The size and economic output of the common European market make the EU a major player in the global economy. The IMF is expecting growth of 2.2 percent for 2018 in Euroland, which has 19 member states. As the strongest economy in the EU, Germany has a particular responsibility, not least of all at times of economic and social change. This was evidenced during the financial and sovereign debt crisis. The EMU member states set up the European Stabilisation Mechanism (ESM) as a rescue fund. In close partnership with France and the other member states, the Federal Government seeks to further strengthen and reform Euroland to enable the euro to withstand crises better.

Franco-German friendship – the driving force behind European unification

Parallel to European integration, after the Second World War France and Germany established a close partnership, which now-

NUMBER

512 million

people live in the 28 member states of the European Union. This gives it the third-largest population after China and India. Its citizens speak 24 languages and live in an area covering four million square kilometres. GDP totals 15.33 trillion euros. With a share of 15.6 percent of the world's exports and 14.8 percent of imports, the EU places second behind China and the USA respectively.

→ **europa.eu**

The EU has successfully grown from six to 28 members in seven expansions since 1957

adays is often regarded as a model for reconciliation between two peoples. In 1957, both countries were amongst the six founding members of the European Economic Community (EEC), the core of today's EU. Franco-German friendship, substantiated by the 1963 Elysée Treaty, is nurtured by close relations between the civil societies and numerous Franco-German institutions. With regard to European and foreign policy issues, both countries cooperate closely and through joint initiatives repeatedly play a role in constructively advancing European policy.

German-Polish collaboration is a more recent element in the European unification process. In the 1970s, Federal Chancellor Willy Brandt's Ostpolitik achieved initial successes in reconciliation with Poland. ▸

▸ This was continued by the recognition of the two countries' common border in the Two Plus Four Treaty on the external aspects of German Unity in 1990, and with the Border Treaty concluded the same year and institutionalised in the 1991 German-Polish Treaty on Good Neighbourliness. The close relationships with France and Poland are nurtured in the trilateral format of the Weimar Triangle.

More global weight through joint European action

The 2009 Treaty of Lisbon institutionalised the Common Foreign and Security Policy (CFSP) still further. The EU High Representative for Foreign Affairs and Security Policy, who chairs the Council of Foreign Ministers, is also Vice-President of the European Commission. Italian Federica Mogherini has held this office since 2014. She is also responsible for representing the EU externally on all CFSP issues. The European External Action Service (EEAS) assists the High Representative in discharging her duties. Through these institutional changes the EU has considerably strengthened its visibility and efficacy outside its own territory. The Common Security and Defence Policy (CSDP) gives the EU the necessary operational abilities to ensure effective crisis management. Civilian and military means are brought to bear. The long-term idea is to create a European Security and Defence Union (ESDU).

The influx of refugees and migrants above all in 2015 and 2016 into Europe is a pan-European issue for which Germany with its partners is seeking an enduring answer. The EU Commission's "European Migration Agenda" has already achieved firm results with measures such as the EU-Turkey Declaration of March 2016, migration partnerships with African home or transit countries, and the battle against human traffickers: In 2017 the number of irregular border crossings on key migration routes fell 63-percent on the 2016 figure. The question

MILESTONES

1957
The European unification process begins. The signing of the Treaty of Rome by Belgium, Germany, France, Italy, Luxembourg, and the Netherlands marks the foundation of the European Economic Community (EEC).

1979
Europeans vote together. The Members of the European Parliament, which sits in Strasbourg and Brussels, are directly elected for the first time. They had previously been delegated by the national parliaments.

1993
Europe's union becomes tangible for its citizens. In Schengen in Luxembourg, Germany, France, and the Benelux countries agree to end internal border controls. Other countries follow.

European partners: Federal Chancellor Angela Merkel and French President Emmanuel Macron

of the more just distribution of asylum seekers in the EU still requires a sustainable, fair answer, however.

Germany is working intensely in the areas of crisis prevention and humanitarian assistance to combat the causes that force people to flee their countries. Information plays a key role and the Federal Foreign Office and the foreign missions in crisis regions outline the dangers of flight and irregular migration and thus try to counteract the deliberate false information provided by criminal human traffickers.

In the second half of 2020 it will be Germany's turn to hold the EU Council Presidency and it intends to set emphases in crucial political fields. ■

2002

Europe gives itself a currency. In initially 12 EU member states, the cash euro is introduced; it had served as book money since 1999. The new European Central Bank (ECB) is based in Frankfurt am Main.

2004

On 1 May Estonia, Latvia, Lithuania, Poland, Czech Republic, Slovakia, Slovenia, Hungary, Malta, and Cyprus join the EU. Bulgaria and Romania follow three years later; Croatia in 2013.

2009

The EU presents a united front in the world. With the Treaty of Lisbon, the EU creates the office of the High Representative for Foreign Affairs and Security Policy. A European External Action Service (EEAS) is established.

TOPIC

PROTECTION OF HUMAN RIGHTS

"Human dignity shall be inviolable. To respect and protect it shall be the duty of all state authority." This is the clear mandate in Article 1 of the German Basic Law, in which Germany acknowledges "inviolable and inalienable human rights" as "the basis of every community, of peace and of justice in the world". Germany also takes this obligation seriously in its relations with foreign countries. The protection and strengthening of human rights play a special role in the foreign-policy and international context, as systematic human rights violations are frequently the first step towards conflicts and crises. Together with its partners in the EU and in collaboration with the United Nations (UN), Germany advocates the protection and improvement of human rights standards.

INFO

Civil Society The many non-government organisations in Germany also champion the global enforcement of human rights, progress in development policy, and humanitarian assistance. They encourage the politicians responsible to take action and raise awareness for such activities among the population. But they also take active steps themselves, collect donations and coordinate projects of their own. Around 120 organisations make up VENRO, the umbrella organisation of non-governmental development organisations.
→ venro.org

Commitment to international human rights institutions

Germany is a contracting party to the UN's important human rights treaties and their Additional Protocols (Civil Pact, Social Pact, Anti-Racism Convention, Women's Rights Convention, Convention against Torture, Children's Rights Convention, Convention on the Rights of Persons with Disabilities, Convention for the Protection of All Persons from Enforced Disappearance). Most recently Germany signed the Additional Protocol to the Convention against Torture, and the Convention on the Rights of Persons with Disabilities, both of which have been in force since 2009. Germany was the first European nation to ratify the Additional Protocol to the Children's Rights Convention, which makes an individual complaints procedure possible.

The Federal Government supports protection from discrimination and racism, takes an active stand worldwide against the death penalty and for political participation and legal protection, defends the freedom of religion and belief, fights human trafficking, and pushes for enforcement of the right to housing and the right to clean water and sanitation. 2.1 billion people worldwide

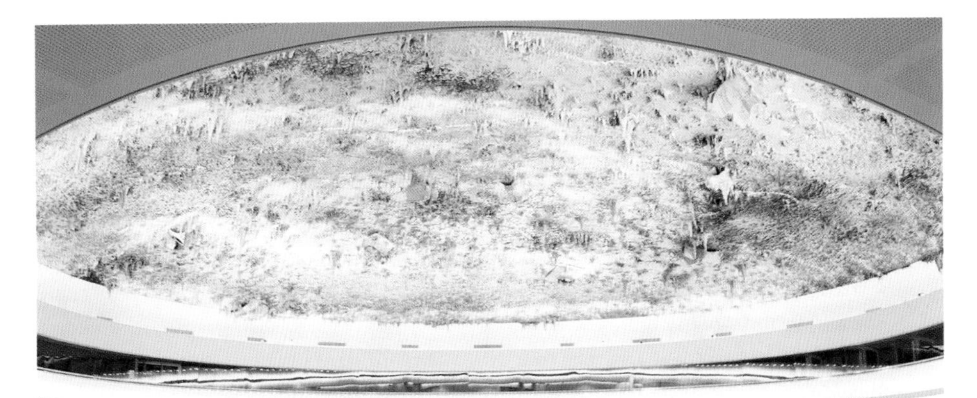

The Human Rights Council in Geneva is the United Nations' most important human rights committee

have no access to clean water. Germany, as one of the largest donors in this sector, is helping to change this situation by spending 400 million euros annually on several projects. Access to water, one of the more recent human rights issues, is a key focal point of German development cooperation. In Africa alone, by 2017 access to water supplies had thus been created for 25 million people.

Germany was a member of the UN Human Rights Council in Geneva, Switzerland, from 2013-5 and from 2016-8. The Human Rights Council's most important tool is the Universal Periodic Review, which provides all UN member states with an opportunity to declare what actions they have taken to fulfil their human rights obligations, and answer critical questions. Germany underwent this procedure in 2018 for the third time. ▸

▸ **Germany is one** of the most active countries on the European Council, which has 47 member states and champions the protection and promotion of human rights, the rule of law, and democracy throughout Europe. With landmark conventions, in particular the European Human Rights Convention, the European Council plays a strong role in establishing a common European judicial area and monitors adherence to binding common standards and values on the European continent.

International human rights policy tools

The European Court of Human Rights (ECtHR) in Strasbourg, France is one of the European Council's main institutions for enforcing human rights in Europe. Each and every citizen of the 47 member states of the European Council can resort directly to the ECtHR with complaints concerning a violation of rights protected by the European Human Rights Convention. Germany emphatically advocates that all member states of the European Council accept and implement the decisions of the ECtHR. The International Criminal Court (ICC) in The Hague, the Netherlands, is responsible for the prosecution under international criminal law of serious international crimes such as war crimes, crimes against humanity, and genocide. Germany is in favour of universal recognition of the ECtHR.

The Federal Government Commissioner for Human Rights Policy and Humanitarian Aid, Bärbel Kofler, is based in the Federal Foreign Office. She observes international developments, coordinates human rights activities with other state bodies, and advises the Federal Foreign Minister. The German parliament, the Bundestag, has accompanied and monitored German human rights policy since 1998 through its Committee for Human Rights and Humanitarian Aid. In 2000, the German Institute for Human Rights, a state-funded but independent body, was established in Berlin. As a national human rights institution as defined in the UN's Paris

DIAGRAM

Cooperation and development
Germany is not only one of the important and major donor countries in the field of government development cooperation; it is also an important donor for, and actively helps shape humanitarian aid.

Spending on government development cooperation in USD billion (2017)

Country	USD billion
USA	35.26
Germany	24.68
Great Britain	17.94
Japan	11.48
France	11.36

Source: Preliminary figures, status April 2018, OECD / DAC

Principles, it is intended to help the promotion and protection of human rights by Germany at home and abroad.

Humanitarian aid for people in acute need

Through its humanitarian aid worldwide the Federal Government helps people in acute need as a result of natural disasters, armed conflicts, or other crises and conflicts – or where there is a risk of this becoming the case. It is not about the causes of their plight. Humanitarian aid is an expression of ethical responsibility and solidarity with people in need. It is geared to the requirements of the needy and is based on the humanitarian principles of humanity, neutrality, impartiality, and independence.

Germany assumes responsibility globally for people in distress and actively advocates strengthening and advancing the international humanitarian system. In 2017, given the ever growing need, the Federal Government provided budgetary resources of some 1.75 billion euros for humanitarian aid. The Federal Government does not provide this directly, but supports suitable projects conducted by the UN's humanitarian organisations, the Red Cross and Red Crescent Movement, and German non-government organisations. Moreover, Germany is a long-standing supporter and second-largest donor to the UN's Central Emergency Response Fund and the UN's humanitarian community funds for countries.

The protection of human rights is also an important field of activity for cyber foreign policy. In 2013 and 2014 the UN General Assembly passed resolutions on the right to privacy in the digital age. They were on the back of a German-Brazilian initiative. Germany is of the opinion that human rights online are just as valid as offline. In 2018 Germany emphasised its commitment to protecting personal privacy in the cyber age and assumed the chair of the Freedom Online Coalition, which champions promoting human rights in the digital age. ■

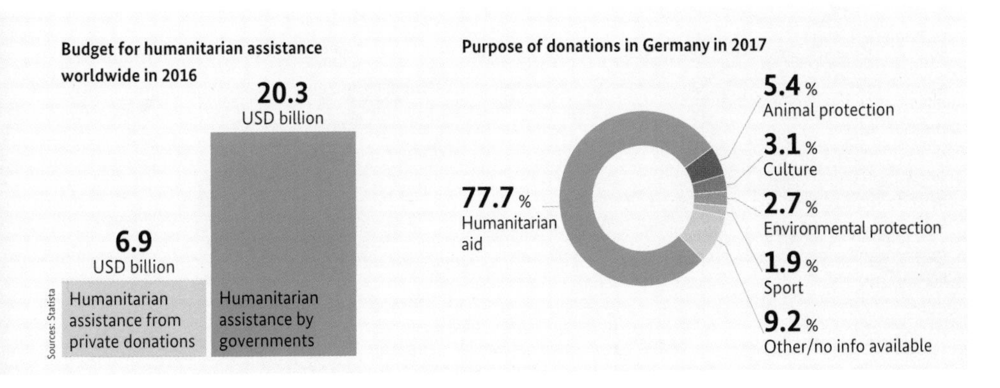

PANORAMA

OPEN NETWORK PARTNER

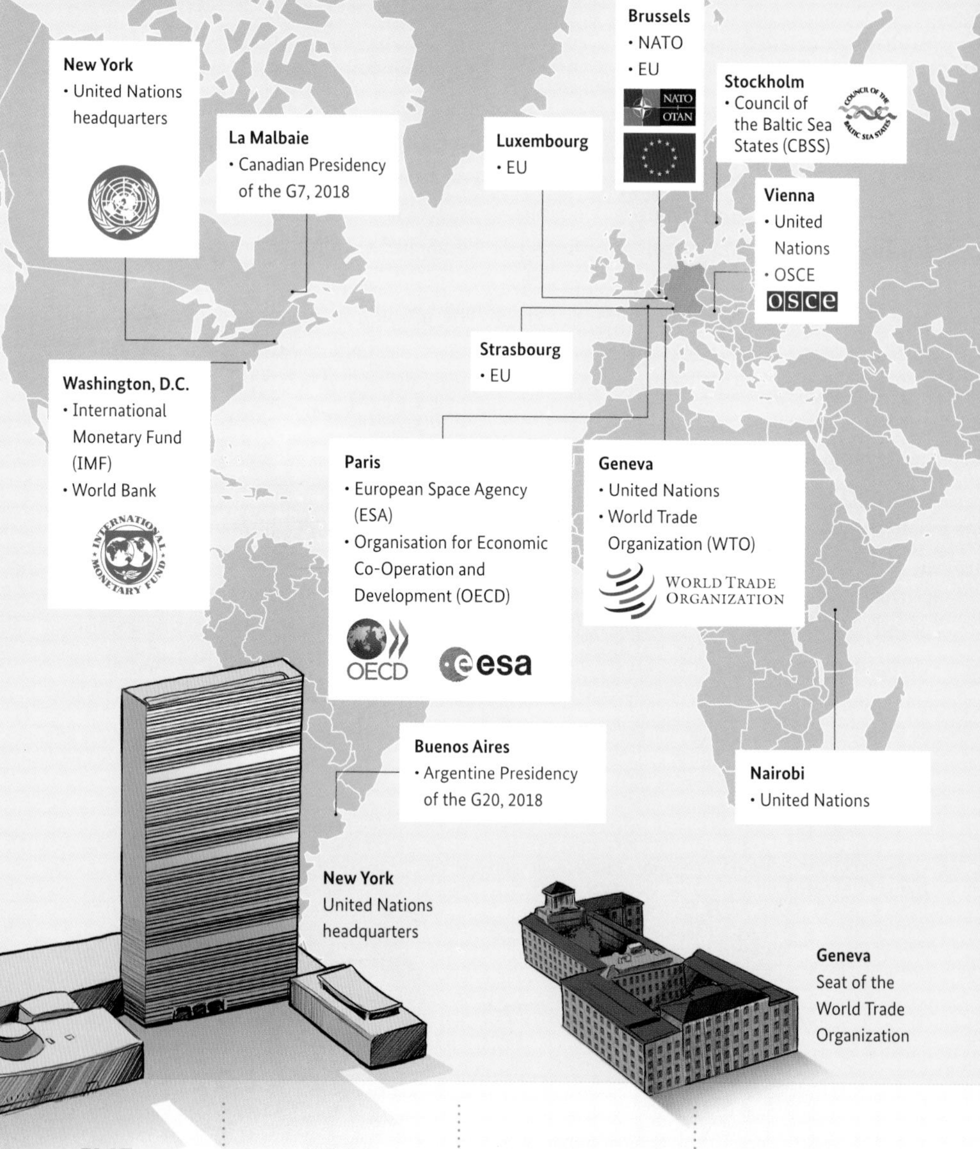

IMF
Germany has been a member of the International Monetary Fund since 1952

NATO
Germany has been a member of the North Atlantic Treaty Organization since 1955

EU
Germany has been a member of what is today the EU since it was founded in 1957

UN
Germany became a member of the United Nations in 1973

The United Nations (UN) in Germany

Berlin
- International Labour Organization (ILO) – office in Germany
- International Organization for Migration (IOM) – Germany
- The United Nations High Commissioner for Refugees (UNHCR) – Regional Representation for Germany and Austria
- World Food Programme (WFP) – liaison office in Germany
- Office of the World Bank in Berlin
- UNICEF Office Berlin

Bonn UN Campus
- Secretariat for the United Nations Convention to Combat Desertification (UNCCD)
- Secretariat for the United Nations Framework Convention on Climate Change (UNFCCC)
- United Nations Volunteers (UNV)
- United Nations SDG Action Campaign
- United Nations System Staff College (UNSSC)
- International Strategy for Disaster Reduction/Platform for the Promotion of Early Warning (UN/ISDR-PPEW)
- United Nations University Vice Rectorate in Europe (UNU-ViE)
- and 12 other UN agencies

Dresden
- United Nations University – Institute for Integrated Management of Material Fluxes and of Resources (UNU-FLORES)

Frankfurt am Main
- International Finance Corporation (IFC), World Bank Group

Hamburg
- International Tribunal for the Law of the Sea (ITLOS)
- UNESCO Institute for Lifelong Learning (UIL)

Munich
- United Nations World Food Programme (WFP)– Innovation Accelerator

Nuremberg
- UNHCR Nuremberg branch

Hamburg
International Tribunal for the Law of the Sea

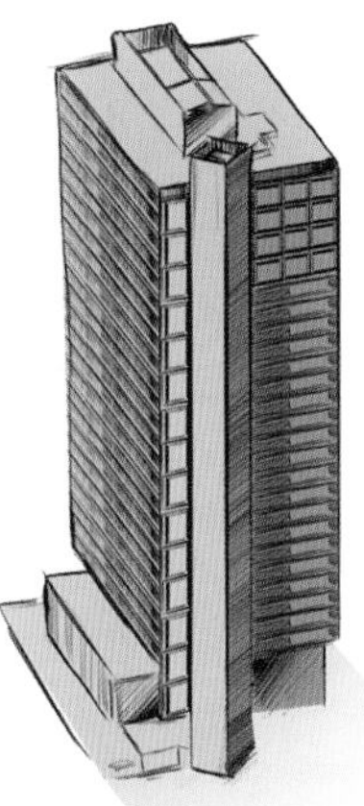

Bonn
The “Tall Eugene” building on the UN Campus

Strasbourg
European Parliament

OSCE
Germany has been a member of what is today the OSCE since 1975

G7
Germany has been a member of the informal bloc since it was founded in 1975

WTO
Germany has been a member of the World Trade Organization since 1995

G20
Germany has been a member of the Group of Twenty since it was founded in 1999 in Berlin

TOPIC

SUSTAINABLE DEVELOPMENT

German development policy is geared as a cornerstone of a global structural and peace policy to helping improve living conditions in partner countries. It aims to overcome hunger and poverty worldwide and strengthen democracy and the rule of law. The Federal Ministry of Economic Cooperation and Development draws up the guidelines and concepts. As part of government development cooperation, Germany works with 85 partner countries in jointly agreed country programmes that can involve all the various government tools for development cooperation. Africa is a key region, but Germany also works extremely closely with countries in Asia, southeast Europe, and Latin America.

In 2016 Germany for the first time achieved the goal set by the United Nations of investing 0.7 percent of gross domestic product in development cooperation. On an international scale, Germany with an annual 24.68 billion dollars is the second-largest donor country for public development cooperation after the USA. In the various country projects are managed by implementing organisations, as a rule Deutsche Gesellschaft für Internationale Zusammenarbeit (GIZ) and the KfW Group, and also others.

The 2030 Agenda for Sustainable Development

Global development in the coming years will be decisively influenced by the 2030 Agenda as resolved by the 70th Session of the UN General Assembly at the end of September 2015. The core of the Agenda 2030 are the 17 ambitious Sustainable Development Goals (SDGs). Global realisation of the Agenda can lay the foundations for global economic progress in harmony with social justice and within Earth's ecological limits.

Pursuit of the Millennium Development Goals (MDGs) in 2000-15 succeeded in halving poverty worldwide and, amongst other things, improving access to drinking water and education. From 2012-6, the number of the most impoverished people among the world's population fell from 12.8 percent to 9.6 percent despite adjustments to the baseline defining absolute poverty from 1.25 to 1.90 US dollars a day. The major goal of eliminating extreme poverty by 2030 thus seems possible. Problems such as the overly great use of resources, ongoing climate change and the destruction of the environment, high unemployment and social inequality, remain urgent. The Agenda 2030 will boost a worldwide change in favour of more sustainability – in the economic, ecological, and social dimensions, and taking the existing links between the three into consideration. It is meant as a "future agreement" for the world applicable to all countries and addressing a broad range of policies that go far beyond development cooperation: In addition to the fight against starvation and poverty, planet Earth, as the basis of existence

The United Nations' 2030 Agenda aims to advance sustainable development in important areas for the future

of future generations, will be protected; economic systems and lifestyles will become more just and more sustainable (as well as more efficient), discrimination will be fought, not least of all by strengthening effective inclusive and democratic institutions, responsible governance, as well as the rule of law. Ultimately the agreement for ensuring sustainability in the future needs a "multi-player" approach: The plan envisages that in addition to governments, above all social groups and the worlds of business and scholarship play important roles in the implementation of Agenda 2030. ■

BUSINESS & INNOVATION

A Strong Hub • Global Player • Lead Markets and Innovative Products • Sustainable Economy • Digital Revolution • A Valued Trading Partner • Attractive Labour Market

INSIGHT

A STRONG HUB

Germany is the largest economy in the European Union (EU) and the fourth largest in the world after the USA, China, and Japan. The German economy has its great innovativeness and strong focus on exports to thank for its competitiveness and global networking. In high-selling sectors, such as car-making, mechanical and plant engineering, the chemicals industry and medical technology, exports account for well over half of total sales. In 2016, only China and the USA exported more goods. Germany invests 92 billion euros annually in research and development (R&D). Many companies are well on the way to "Industry 4.0", a project destined in particular to advance digitisation in production engineering and logistics.

The positive economic momentum has led to a favourable trend on the labour market. Germany is one of the countries with the highest employment rates in the EU and is the country with the lowest youth unemployment percentage. This underscores the value of dual vocational training, which has become an export commodity in its own right and is being adapted by many countries. Factors such as the availability of skilled labour, infrastructure, and legal certainty are further characteristics of Germany, which is very high on the list in many international rankings. Peter Altmaier (CDU) heads the Federal Ministry for Economic Affairs and Energy.

Since 1949 the idea of a social market economy has formed the basis of German economic policy. The social market economy guarantees free entrepreneurial activity while at the same time endeavouring to create social checks and balances. Formulated in the post-War years by Ludwig Erhard, who ▸

VIDEO AR APP

Business & Innovation: the video on the topic → **tued.net/en/vid3**

Industry 4.0: the economy in Germany is fast en route to the digitised future

was later to become Federal Chancellor, the concept has kept Germany's economic development on a successful track. Germany actively engages in shaping globalisation and champions a sustainable global economic system, which offers fair opportunities to everyone.

Germany is one of the 12 countries which introduced the euro in 2002. The financial market crisis (2008) and the subsequent debt crisis affected the whole of the Eurozone, Germany included. To combat adverse impacts, the Federal Government employed a twin-track strategy, which involved not taking on any new debt and adopting measures to bolster innovativeness. For the first time since 1969, the government has been able to present a balanced federal budget since 2014.

Accounting for more than 99 percent of all companies, small and medium-sized enterprises (SMEs) are the backbone of the economy. They supplement the corporations listed primarily on the DAX index at the Frankfurt Stock Exchange, the most important financial centre in Continental Europe. The European Central Bank, which as an EU institution among other things guards the euro's price stability, is also headquartered in Frankfurt am Main. ■

INTERNET

Federal Ministry for Economic Affairs and Energy (BMWi)
Priority issues and initiatives
→ **bmwi.de**

Employment Agency
Labour market data and job vacancies
→ **arbeitsagentur.de**

Virtual Welcome Center
Point of contact for international jobseekers with information on jobs in Germany
→ **arbeitsagentur.de**

Financial centre with a long-standing tradition: Frankfurt am Main is Germany's most important stock exchange

COMPACT

PLAYERS & ORGANISATIONS

Federation of German Industries
The Federation of German Industries (BDI) represents the interests of over 100,000 industrial companies. It has an extensive network in all important markets and in international organisations.
→ **bdi.eu**

German Chambers of Commerce Abroad
The German Chambers of Commerce Abroad (AHK), delegations and representative offices of German industry and commerce, form a network with 130 locations in 90 countries.
→ **ahk.de**

German diplomatic missions
The 227 embassies and consulates, together with the AHK and Germany Trade and Invest (GTAI), are the third pillar in the promotion of foreign trade.
→ **auswaertiges-amt.de**

Association of German Chambers of Commerce and Industry
The Association of German Chambers of Commerce and Industry (DIHK) is the umbrella organisation of the 80 German Chambers of Commerce and Industry; a total of 3.6 million commercial enterprises are members.
→ **dihk.de**

German Institute for Economic Research
The German Institute for Economic Research (DIW) in Berlin is the biggest of the numerous German economic research institutes.
→ **diw.de**

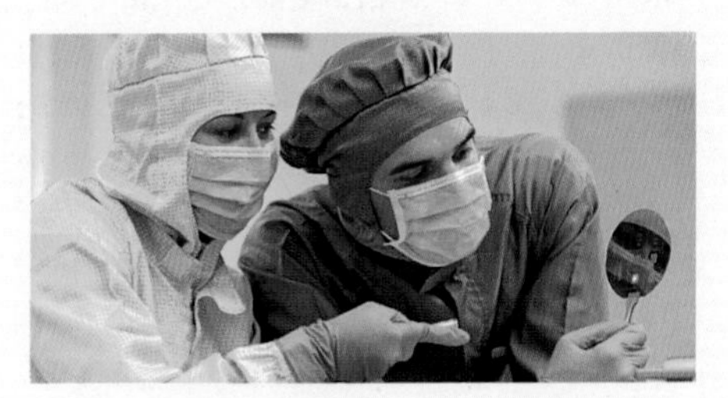

Germany Trade and Invest
Germany Trade and Invest (GTAI) is the economic development agency of the Federal Republic of Germany. With over 50 locations worldwide it helps German companies set up operations abroad, promotes Germany as a business and technology location and helps foreign companies settle in Germany.
→ **gtai.de**

Council for Sustainable Development
Appointed by the Federal Government, the Council for Sustainable Development is responsible among other things for developing measures to implement the National Sustainability Strategy.
→ **nachhaltigkeitsrat.de**

DIGITAL PLUS
More information about all the topics in the chapter – annotated link lists, articles, documents, speeches; plus more in-depth information about topics such as the social market economy, dual vocational training, economic policy, the European economic and financial crisis. → **tued.net/en/dig3**

TOPIC

GLOBAL PLAYER

Germany is an industrialised nation with strong international links and a pronounced export focus. In the annual World Trade Organization (WTO) rankings, Germany regularly places among the three largest exporters behind China and the USA. In 2017, the foreign trade balance closed with a surplus of 245 billion euros. Exports by German companies (goods and services) amounted to 1,279 billion euros, with the value of imports totalling 1,034 billion euros. Germany is strongly integrated in the global economy and benefits from free trade and open markets. The World Economic Forum's "Global Competitive Index 2017-2018" ranks Germany fifth in the list of the most competitive countries. In all, 137 economies were rated.

Every second euro earned in Germany is generated through an international business transaction. Almost one job in four is dependent on exports; in industry it is even one in two. Over one million companies engage in foreign trade. In 2015, 720,000 corporations imported goods from other countries, while approximately 360,000 were busy as exporters. Some 10,700 firms domiciled outside Germany played a significant role in German foreign trade; the Association of German Chambers of Commerce and Industry (DIHK) estimates that more than 7 million employees work for German companies abroad.

In terms of exports, the emphasis is on motor vehicles and automotive components, machines, chemical products, and IT appliances and electronic products. These four product groups account for a good half of German exports. Overall, the export ratio has since 1991 almost doubled, rising from 23.7 percent to 47.3 percent. In 2017 the ▸

DIAGRAM

Economic leadership
German companies have an excellent international reputation. They stand for "Made in Germany", a quality seal held in high esteem worldwide. The world's fourth-largest economic power, Germany has a pronounced export focus.

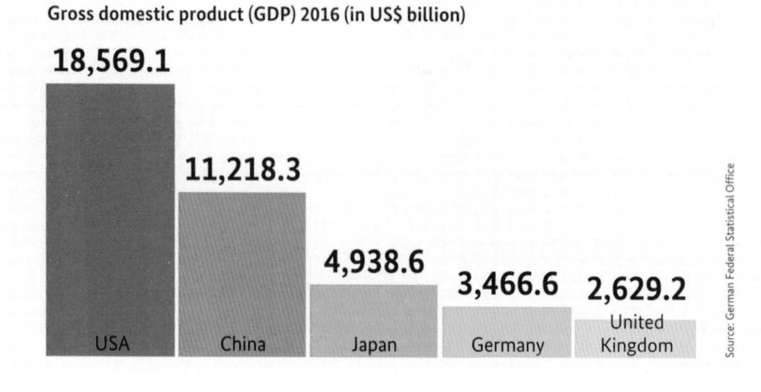

Containers – a symbol of globalisation: Hamburg docks is a major transhipment point

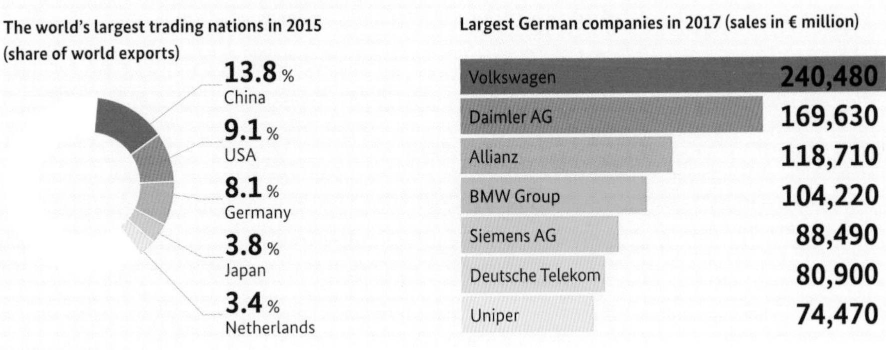

foreign trade ratio, i.e., the sum total of imports and exports in relation to the gross domestic product (GDP), stood at 86.9 percent. This makes Germany's economy the "most open" of the G7 countries. By way of comparison, in 2015 the USA had a foreign trade ratio of 28 percent.

The partner countries in the European Union (EU) are the most important market for German goods and attract 56 percent of all exports. France is traditionally Germany's largest export market, though since 2015 the USA has headed the list, followed by the People's Republic of China, the Netherlands, and Great Britain. With regard to imports, however, the rankings run the other way round: In 2017 most imports came from China, the Netherlands, France, the USA, and Italy. Although in some cases growth rates are weakening, nevertheless economic and trade relations with Asian countries are becoming ever more important and today 5,000 German companies have investments in China alone.

GLOBAL

OECD Economic Outlook Twice a year in its Economic Outlook, the Organisation for Economic Co-operation and Development (OECD) analyses the most important trends and the prospects for the next two years in the 34 OECD member countries and emerging nations. The overall assumption is that the global economy will grow by 3.5% in 2018. This would be the highest rate recorded since 2010. Growth is expected to weaken again in 2019.
→ **oecd.org**

German direct investments abroad, which since 1990 have increased fivefold to over one trillion euros (2015), are an expression of its strong links within the global economy. A fifth of the total was invested in Euroland. On the other hand, some 80,000 foreign companies employ more than 3.7 million people in Germany. The value of foreign direct investments stands at 466 billion euros.

The trade-fair industry is regarded as the hub of world trade. Germany is the leading trade-fair centre when it comes to organising and staging international trade fairs. Two thirds of globally important industry events are held in Germany. Every year, 10 million visitors attend around 150 international trade fairs and exhibitions.

At the same time Germany is a transhipment hub for the flow of goods in Europe and the world as a whole. More goods transit through Germany than through any other EU country. About a third of the turnover in the ten most important logistics markets in the EU is generated in Germany, with 3 million people involved in logistics. The Port of Hamburg, where around 9 million standard containers are processed each year, is a gateway to the world.

Commitment to fair and free global trade

Germany supports open markets and fair, free trade based on clear and reliable regulations. Among other things, the country pursues these goals with the three pillars for the promotion of foreign trade. These include 227 German diplomatic missions abroad, 130 German Chambers of Commerce Abroad (AHK), delegations, and representative offices of the German economy in 90 countries, and Germany Trade and Invest (GTAI), the economic development agency of the Federal Republic of Germany. They all help small and medium-sized enterprises penetrate new markets and endeavour to improve framework conditions.

Germany is involved in shaping globalisation in various ways, be it through formulating regulations for international trade, regulating financial markets, or managing cash and foreign currency. Given failed multilateral negotiations (the Doha Development Round), close attention is being paid to bilateral EU free trade agreements. The EU-Canada Comprehensive Economic and Trade Agreement (CETA) entered into force in 2017 and negotiations on a free trade agreement with Japan have been concluded; the only thing not yet agreed upon is investment protection. The EU Free Trade Agreement with South Korea, the first with an Asian country, has been in force since 2011; since that time exports to South Korea have risen each year by some 10 percent. In 2015 the EU and Vietnam adopted a free trade agreement, the first of its kind between the EU and a developing country. ■

Global market hubs: as many as 10 million visitors attend the major trade fairs annually

TOPIC

LEAD MARKETS AND INNOVATIVE PRODUCTS

Germany's economic prowess is decidedly based on its industrial performance and its capacity for innovation. With 775,000 jobs, the automotive industry in particular is regarded as a showcase discipline with regard to the Made in Germany seal of quality. With its six strong brands, namely Volkswagen, BMW, Daimler, and the VW-owned marques Audi and Porsche, as well as Opel (Groupe PSA), the automotive industry is one of the forces driving the global mobility sector.

The companies invest billions in research and development (R&D) to shore up their competitive edge. Electronic and digital networking, as well as assisted or self-driving cars, are the megatrends for automobiles. In global terms, in 2017 the German carmakers, which have a major share in the middle and luxury car segments, produced some 16.45 million cars, with two out of three cars by German manufacturers being made abroad.

Alongside the automotive industry, plant and mechanical engineering and the chemical industry are traditionally strong pillars of the German economy. Founded in 1865 and headquartered in Ludwigshafen, BASF, which has a payroll of 115,000 employees working at 353 production sites in more than 80 countries, is the world's largest chemicals company. Key sectors also include the electrical and electronic engineering industry, with global player Siemens active in 190 countries. Its application solutions, from mobility to renewable energies, are regarded as highly innovative. The fact that the major sectors of industry achieve export ratios of 60 percent and more indicates just how important the global market is for them.

The most important economic centres in Germany are the Ruhr Area, Greater Munich and Greater Stuttgart (high-tech, automotive construction), Rhine-Neckar (chemicals, IT), Frankfurt am Main (finance), Cologne and Hamburg (port, aircraft construction, media). In east Germany, small but efficient high-tech centres have emerged, in particular in the "beacon regions" of Dresden, Jena, Leipzig, Leuna, and Berlin-Brandenburg.

Automotive groups head and dominate the list of the biggest German companies (by 2016 sales): Volkswagen comes first, with Daimler and BMW following in second and fourth place respectively. Allianz (insurance) is in third place and Siemens (electrotechnology) fifth, ahead of Deutsche Telekom and Uniper, spun-off from energy group Eon.

Industry in Germany specialises in the development and manufacture of complex goods, in particular capital goods and

Successful the world over: German car manufacturers are among the big players in the global mobility sector

innovative production technologies. Industry carries far more weight in Germany than in many other economies. A total of 7.27 million people work in industry and manufacturing. Only in South Korea is the share of manufacturing in gross value added higher.

The economy's capacity for innovation is regarded as the driving force behind Germany's economic strength. The step-up in R&D activities since 2007 has spurred trends. Both business and the public sector played a role in this; the Federal Government's High-Tech Strategy has been a key stimulus here. In 2016 a total of 92 billion euros was spent on R&D in Germany, which corresponds to a 2.93-percent share of gross domestic product (GDP). This puts Germany in fifth place among comparable OECD countries, ahead of the USA and well ahead of France and Great Britain. Of Ger- ▸

many's main rivals, only South Korea and Japan invested more in R&D. Germany is considered to be Europe's champion inventor. In 2016 German companies filed around 32,000 applications for patent protection to the European Patent Office in Munich. The same year, 67,898 inventions were registered with the German Patent and Trade Mark Office (DPMA) – a new record. The automotive supplier Bosch, with 3,693 registrations, and the Schaeffler Group (2,316), which likewise operates in the automotive components sector, were the most prolific. In total there were exactly 129,511 German patents in force in 2016. Including patents granted by the European Patent Office, a total of 615,404 patents were valid in Germany in 2016.

Today, it is hard to imagine Germany as an industrial centre without its services economy, which has long been on a constant growth curve. A good 80 percent of all companies operate in this sector, accounting for almost 70 percent of gross domestic product and three quarters of all jobs. Of around 30 million people in gainful employment, 12 million work for public or private service providers, almost 10 million in retailing, hospitality and transportation, and more than five million for corporate service providers.

Small and medium-sized enterprises – the heart of the economy

Despite the numerous global players and large flagship businesses, the German economy is characterised by 3.6 million small and medium-sized enterprises (SMEs), as well as countless self-employed persons and freelancers. The SME segment includes around 99.6 percent of companies. SMEs are defined as firms with annual sales of less than 50 million euros and fewer than 500 employees. Numerous companies founded by entrepreneurially minded migrants now also enjoy SME status. More than 700,000 people with a migrant background own a company. As such, migrants in Germany are an important economic factor.

MILESTONES

1955
On 5 August the one millionth VW Beetle leaves the assembly line in Wolfsburg. An absolute top seller, the car becomes a symbol of what went down in history as the Economic Miracle.

1969
In Toulouse (France) the Airbus consortium is founded as a Franco-German joint venture. Today, Airbus S.A.S. is the world's second-largest aircraft manufacturer.

1989
Postal Reform I marks the beginning of the privatisation of the giant publicly owned corporation that is Deutsche Bundespost. The privatisation is regarded as one of the biggest reforms in German economic history.

According to studies by the KfW Banking Group, overall there is a decline in the number of innovative companies – only 22 percent of SMEs invest in innovative products and processes. It is above all a few larger medium-sized companies that are responsible for innovation efforts. In numerous niche market segments, German SMEs are frequently hidden champions, with leaders offering highly innovative products in European and global markets. The creative industry has become firmly established in the fabric of the economy. Frequently in small, under-capitalised companies it plays a pioneering role on the way to a digital, knowledge-based economy, and is regarded as a significant source of ideas for innovative products. With more than 30,000 such firms registered, the Berlin-Brandenburg area is considered to be an international seedbed for creative industries and start-ups.

The economy is on the threshold of the fourth industrial revolution. Driven by the Internet, the real and virtual worlds are growing together to create an Internet of Things. The Federal Government's aim is for the economy and scientists alike to support the implementation of Industry 4.0 and in so doing position Germany as a leading provider of these technologies and as a future manufacturing hub. ■

INFO

Corporate tax rates

Since the mid-1990s there has been an international trend towards falling corporate tax rates. Germany has long since not been among the high-tax countries. In comparison with other countries, if anything, it even has below-average tax and welfare contribution levels. The average overall tax burden for companies is less than 30 percent. On account of the locally variable trade tax rate, in some regions in Germany it is below 23 percent.

→ gtai.de

1990

The Treuhandanstalt, a government-owned but independent trust agency, begins transforming the socialist planned economy of the former East Germany with its several thousand state-owned enterprises into a market economy.

2002

From 1948 until 1998 the Deutsche Mark is the official currency as "book money", until 2001 as cash. It is replaced on 1 January 2002: Germany and 11 other EU Member States introduce the euro.

2018

In January 2018 the German share index DAX reaches an all-time high of 13,595 points. It reflects the performance of the 30 biggest German companies with the highest sales.

TOPIC

SUSTAINABLE ECONOMY

Germany is one of the world's most sustainable industrialised nations. This is the conclusion reached by an international comparative study of the 34 OECD member states. Against the backdrop of the United Nations' 17 Sustainable Development Goals (SDGs), the countries were systematically analysed for the first time on the basis of 34 indicators ranging from environmental protection and growth to the quality of the welfare systems. Germany was in sixth place, doing well in particular with regard to growth, employment, and social security.

That said, in some areas Germany is far from following a sustainable lifestyle, sustainable business, and a sustainable approach to natural resources. Consequently, in 2017 the Federal Government comprehensively advanced its sustainability strategy and aligned it with the UN's 17 SDGs. The new strategy envisages three levels: measures with an impact in Germany, measures taken by Germany with a global impact, and the direct support of other countries by means of bilateral cooperation.

A growing number of companies in Germany are already making a commitment to society as part of conducting sustainable business. Corporate social responsibility (CSR) primarily hinges on each company's core business, which by dint of globalisation impacts on economic, social and environmental conditions. Most DAX-listed companies as well as many SMEs, institutes, and non-governmental organisations in Germany are members of the United Nations' Global Compact Initiative, founded in 1999. The latter, together with the OECD Guidelines for Multinational Enterprises and the International Labour Organisation's Tripartite Declaration of Principles concerning Multinational Enterprises and Social Policy, form the bedrock of principles on which companies base their CSR efforts. Worldwide, over 9,500 companies from more than 160 countries are members of the voluntary Global Compact Initiative.

The fact that social and ecological responsibility go hand in hand also becomes evident in

LIST

- Biggest company:
  Volkswagen, 642,300 employees
- Biggest bank:
  Deutsche Bank, 97,535 employees
- Most important stock market index:
  Deutscher Aktienindex (DAX)
- Biggest trade fair grounds:
  Hanover
- Biggest aircraft manufacturer:
  Airbus, Hamburg

Decent work: more and more German companies are placing importance on fair standards in global delivery chains

the "Alliance for Sustainable Textiles", which seeks to achieve improvements on both counts for those employed in the textile and clothing industry. 150 German textile manufacturers have joined the initiative launched by the Federal Ministry for Economic Cooperation and Development (BMZ) in 2014. Its members cover around 50% of the German textile market; the goal is to raise that figure to 75%. Considerable improvements have been made on all sides since the fatal accidents in the textile factories in Bangladesh and Pakistan. As of 2018 the Alliance is setting specific standards for all members designed to ensure that the ambitious goals are met. Through the Alliance, Germany documents its pioneering role with regard to international efforts for fair standards in global delivery chains. ■

TOPIC

DIGITAL REVOLUTION

The economy is in the middle of the fourth industrial revolution. Driven by the Internet, through a digital transformation process the real and virtual worlds are becoming increasingly intertwined and together form an Internet of Things. Digitisation represents an historic change for industry and the service economy. The collective term Industry 4.0 embraces solutions, processes and technologies and describes the extensive use of IT and a high degree of system networking in factories. Many German companies champion Industry 4.0, which in particular advances digitisation in the areas of production engineering and logistics.

#NUMBER

714

Internet service providers and other organisations are linked up to DE-CIX. In terms of data throughput, the Internet hub in Frankfurt am Main is the largest in the world. In 2017 data throughput reached the 6-Terabit-per-second mark for the first time. In addition to the Frankfurt hub, DE-CIX operates further Internet hubs in Europe, the Middle East, North America, and India.
→ **de-cix.net**

Overall, industry is expecting ever more intense international competition for leadership in technology. The Federal Government is promoting and actively shaping digital change, and has formulated in the new Coalition Agreement seven ambitious goals, first and foremost developing a "world-class" comprehensive digital infrastructure.

Germany, so the plan, will become the leading provider of Industry 4.0 and the number-one digital growth country in Europe. In positive scenarios, studies estimate additional economic growth potential from Industry 4.0 of between 200 and 425 billion euros by 2025. As a cross-cutting technology, the information and communications technology (ICT) sector plays a key role here. In 2017 it became the largest industrial employer. Over one million employees generate sales of 160 billion euros. The software industry was a particular engine here.

The development of the digital infrastructure is regarded as one of the key tasks in the digitisation drive. The goal: comprehensive development of gigabit networks. Fibre-optic connections are to be installed in every region, in every municipality, ideally up to every building by 2025. This requires telecommunications providers and the state to pull together. The Federal Gov-

Always online: developing the digital infrastructure is among the Federal Government's key projects

ernment is earmarking up to 12 billion euros for this purpose in the current legislative period.

The upcoming 5G generation of mobile communications will play a key role on the path to digitisation. By 2020 some 770 million devices will be networked in Germany alone – alongside smartphones and tablets also vehicles, household appliances, and industrial machines. This poses a challenge above all for mobile connections. The Federal Government aims to make Germany the leading market for 5G. The technology is to be tested in five regions to accelerate development and ensure comprehensive, full coverage. The commercial launch is expected as of 2020. ■

PANORAMA

A VALUED TRADING PARTNER

Key exports by type of goods (2017)

18.3 %
Cars & automotive components

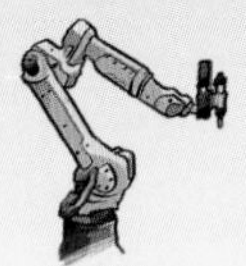

14.4 %
Mechanical equipment

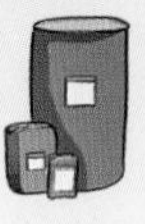

9.0 %
Chemical products

8.6 %
ICT equipment

6.5 %
Electrical equipment

Germany's exports (goods)
by region (2017)

European countries make up Germany's main export market, accounting for 68 percent of German exports. They are followed by the USA, which absorbs 8.7 percent, and China with 6.7 percent.

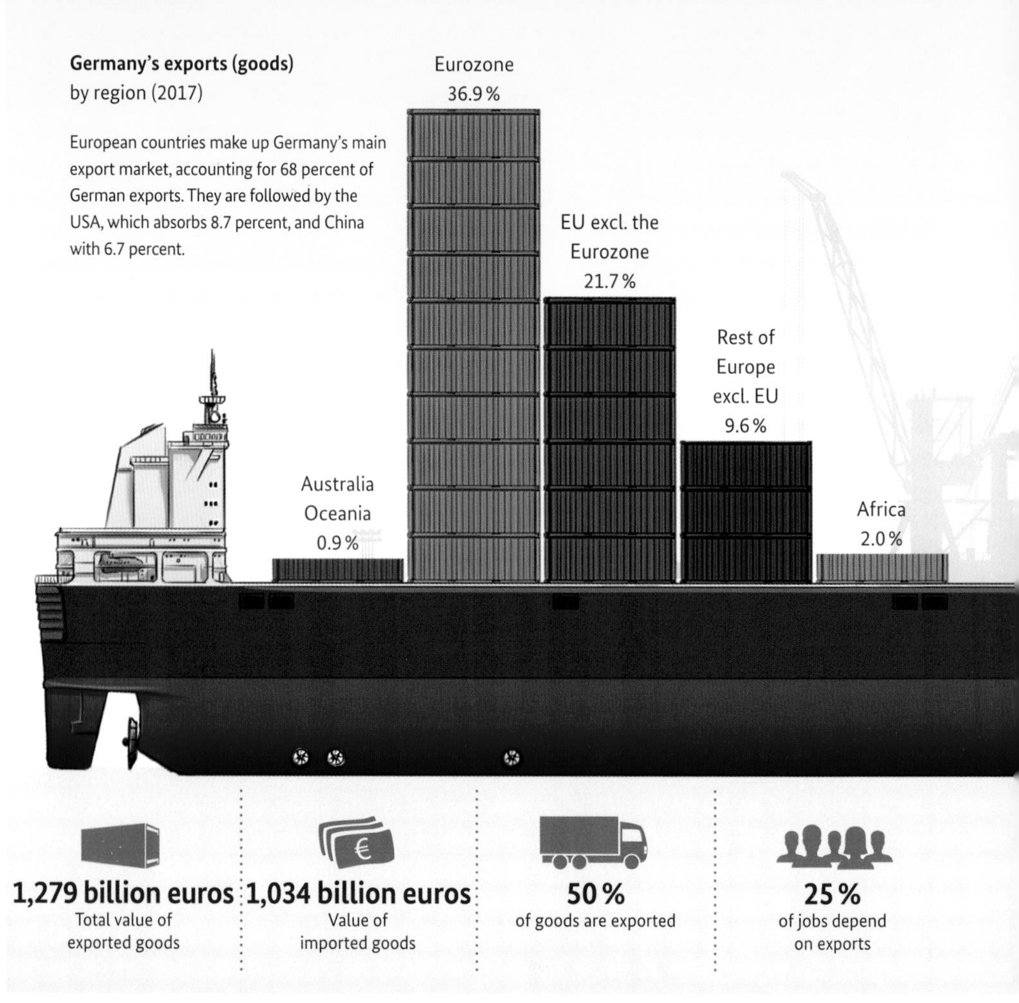

1,279 billion euros
Total value of exported goods

1,034 billion euros
Value of imported goods

50 %
of goods are exported

25 %
of jobs depend on exports

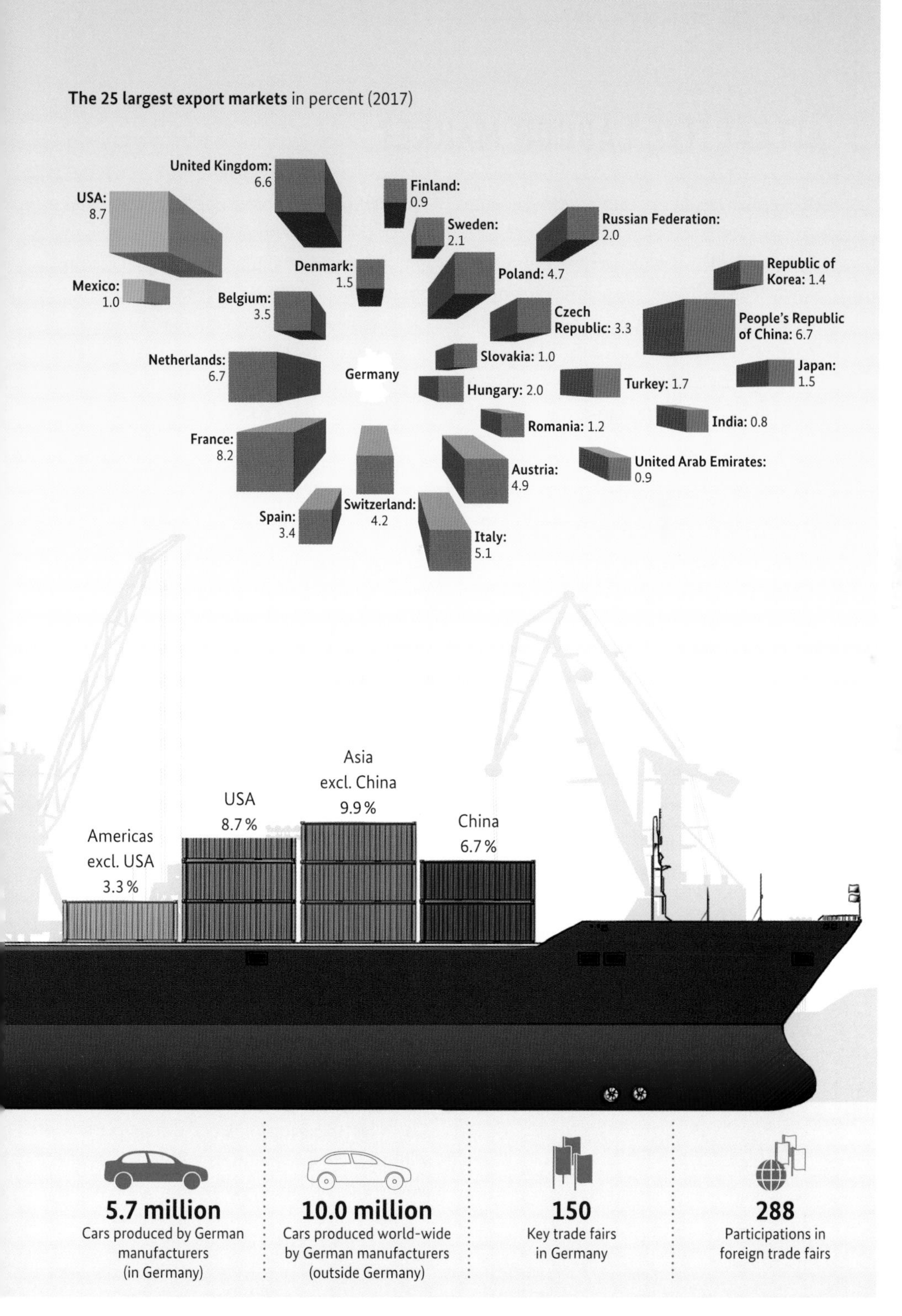

The 25 largest export markets in percent (2017)
United Kingdom: 6.6
USA: 8.7
Finland: 0.9
Sweden: 2.1
Russian Federation: 2.0
Republic of Korea: 1.4
Mexico: 1.0
Denmark: 1.5
Poland: 4.7
Belgium: 3.5
Czech Republic: 3.3
People's Republic of China: 6.7
Netherlands: 6.7
Germany
Slovakia: 1.0
Japan: 1.5
Hungary: 2.0
Turkey: 1.7
Romania: 1.2
India: 0.8
France: 8.2
United Arab Emirates: 0.9
Austria: 4.9
Spain: 3.4
Switzerland: 4.2
Italy: 5.1
Americas excl. USA 3.3 %
USA 8.7 %
Asia excl. China 9.9 %
China 6.7 %
5.7 million
Cars produced by German manufacturers (in Germany)
10.0 million
Cars produced world-wide by German manufacturers (outside Germany)
150
Key trade fairs in Germany
288
Participations in foreign trade fairs

TOPIC

ATTRACTIVE LABOUR MARKET

The German labour market has tended ever upwards in recent years. On an annual average, in 2017 44.3 million people were in gainful employment in Germany. The high employment is an expression of the country's sound economic situation. Germany is one of the EU member states with the lowest unemployment. In 2017 the unemployment rate was on average 5.7 percent, and thus at its lowest level since 1990. This development is borne by a broad-based economy. Firms' demand for new staff is continually rising. As in prior years, in 2017 it was above all employment subject to social insurance contributions that strongly increased. The figures for marginal employment and self-employment continued to fall.

The low level of youth unemployment has drawn the world's attention to the success of dual vocational training, which differs from purely school education. In most countries, the completion of schooling marks the start of working life. Having finished school, almost half of young people in Germany, however, embark on a course of training. These are offered in one of the 350 state-recognised occupations for which accredited vocational training is required within the framework of the dual system. The young people thus receive practical training in their company on three to four weekdays, while on the other day(s) they receive theoretical instruction at a vocational school. Several countries are currently adapting the system of dual vocational training.

With a view to creating a modern, fair, and transparent labour market, the Federal Government has realised numerous projects relating to labour-market policy. Since the beginning of 2015 a statutory minimum wage has been in place. Moreover, the quota for women is intended to ensure equal numbers of men and women in top management positions. Since 2016, listed companies and those that are subject to co-determination regulations have had to adhere to a 30-percent quota for women for seats on the supervisory board. Furthermore, the "Collective Bargaining Act" guarantees that within a company different collective wage agreements do not apply for the same work.

INFO

Make it in Germany - The official online portal for international skilled workers supports people interested in moving to Germany from their arrival to their job search. Experts are also on hand to offer individual advice on visas, recognition of qualifications, and living in Germany – via e-mail, hotline or online chat. Moreover, the portal provides information on the benefits of a training or study programme in Germany in German, English, French, and Spanish.

→ **make-it-in-germany.com**

Dual vocational training: the German model, which combines theory and practice, is being adapted in many countries

What is more, as of 1 July 2014 those who can prove that they have paid social security contributions for 45 years can retire without any deductions at the age of 63.

The Federal Government aspires to achieve full employment. Yet in light of Germany's demographic change, one of the country's most pressing tasks is also to secure its skilled labour base. "Make it in Germany", a multi-language Internet portal for international skilled workers, is a major project designed to open up the labour market. It provides information about career opportunities for those interested in coming to Germany and has current job listings for professions in demand (healthcare, engineering and IT). Furthermore, thanks to the EU Blue Card graduates and skilled workers have easy access to the German labour market. ■

ENVIRONMENT & CLIMATE

A Pioneer in Climate Policy • Innovative Force behind Climate Cooperation • Energy Transition – A Project for Generations • Greentech – A Sector with a Future • Sustainable Energies • Essential Diversity

INSIGHT

A PIONEER IN CLIMATE POLICY

The 21st century is regarded as the "century of the environment". In other words, the extent to which the natural living conditions of future generations on Earth change will be decided in the next decades. A rise in the speed of climate change is primarily regarded as the main danger. Environmental and climate protection have long been a high priority in Germany. Internationally, Germany leads the way in climate protection and is a pioneer in the development of renewable energy sources.

With the changes to the energy sector, referred to as the Energy Transition, Germany is leaving the age of fossil and nuclear energy clearly behind it and heading fast for a future that hinges on sustainable energy sources. This involves a gradual exit from nuclear power by 2022. Furthermore, by 2030 Germany plans to have reduced its greenhouse gas emissions by 55 percent in comparison to the 1990 levels, and is even striving for at least 70 percent by 2040 and 80-95 percent by 2050. In November 2016 the Federal Government was one of the first countries worldwide to specify corresponding climate-policy principles and targets in its "Climate Action Plan 2050". A 28-percent reduction had already been achieved by 2017.

Internationally as well, the Federal Government actively supports environmental protection, cooperation on energy issues, and climate-friendly development. In line with the 2015 Paris Agreement, Germany is committed to limiting global warming to well below 2 degrees Celsius and ideally to 1.5 degrees Celsius. The aim is to achieve broad greenhouse gas emissions neutrality worldwide at the latest in the second half of the century. To this end, emissions of carbon dioxide in the industrialised countries need to be reduced by 80 to 95 percent. Complete "decarbonisation" is ►

VIDEO AR APP

Environment & Climate: the video on the topic → **tued.net/en/vid4**

There is no turning back on the road to the age of renewable energy intended to be achieved before the century is out. The UN Secretariat that monitors the implementation of the framework climate convention is based in the Federal City Bonn.

An intact environment – pure air, clean water, varied nature – is a prerequisite for a high quality of life. Since 1994, environmental protection has been a national objective enshrined in the Basic Law. With regard to air and water quality, indicators have for years now evidenced considerable improvement. There has been a sharp fall in the emission of pollutants such as sulphur dioxide and nitrogen oxides – but there is still room for improvement. There has also been a noticeable drop in the per capita consumption of drinking water – from a peak of 140 to around 120 litres a day.

Germany is pursuing a strategy of combining economic growth and environmental protection with a view to sustainable economics. In addition to the development of renewable energies, the main contributory factors to this are an increase in the efficient use of energy and resources, and the smart use of regenerative raw materials. It a strategy that pays off twofold, because on the one hand the impact on the environment and climate declines, while on the other new fields of business and jobs are created. ■

INTERNET

UNFCCC
Secretariat of the United Nations Framework Convention on Climate Change
→ **unfccc.int**

BMU
Federal Ministry for the Environment, Nature Conservation and Nuclear Safety
→ **bmu.de**

BUND
Bund für Umwelt- und Naturschutz Deutschland/Friends of the Earth Germany → **bund.net**

In Germany, wind power and solar energy are the most important and inexpensive renewable sources of energy

COMPACT

PLAYERS & ORGANISATIONS

Umweltbundesamt

This authority, which is subordinate to the Federal Ministry for the Environment, provides the Federal Government with scientific expertise. The Umweltbundesamt (Federal Environment Agency) is responsible for enforcing environmental laws, for example the marketing approval of chemicals, medication, and pesticides, as well as informing the public about environmental protection.

→ **umweltbundesamt.de**

German Energy Agency

The German Energy Agency (DENA) is a centre of expertise for energy efficiency, renewable energy sources, and intelligent energy systems. It supports the implementation of the Energy Transition and promotes the generation and use of energy in as efficient, safe, cost-effective, and environmentally friendly a way as possible.

→ **dena.de**

Agora Energiewende

The Agora Energiewende think tank sees itself as a forum for dialogue with key stakeholders in the energy policy debate.

→ **agora-energiewende.org**

Potsdam Institute for Climate Impact Research

This institute addresses key scientific issues relating to global climate change and sustainable development.

→ **pik-potsdam.de**

Deutsche Gesellschaft für Internationale Zusammenarbeit

Deutsche Gesellschaft für Internationale Zusammenarbeit (GIZ) is a federal enterprise with worldwide operations. It assists the Federal Government in achieving objectives in the field of development. It advises developing and emerging countries on questions relating to environmental protection, as well as on the just and sustainable use of water as a resource.

→ **giz.de**

Federal Agency for Nature Conservation

The Federal Agency for Nature Conservation (BfN) is responsible for the national and international conservation of nature. Its website features excellent maps of conservation areas.

→ **bfn.de**

DIGITAL PLUS

More information about all the topics in the chapter – annotated link lists, articles, documents, speeches; plus associated terms such as the Framework Convention on Climate Change, greenhouse gas emissions, the Renewable Energy Sources Act, and EU climate protection objectives.

→ **tued.net/en/dig4**

TOPIC

INNOVATIVE FORCE BEHIND CLIMATE COOPERATION

Internationally, Germany has played a pivotal role in putting climate protection on the map. The Federal Government was an innovative force at the Rio de Janeiro Earth Summit as long ago as 1992 and for the 1997 Kyoto Protocol. However, it wasn't until 2015 that a major breakthrough was made, namely with the Paris Agreement. Here 195 countries adopted the very first universal, legally binding global climate protection agreement. The goal is to halt the rise in global average temperature and ideally limit it to 1.5 degrees Celsius. To this end, the states have resolved to reduce or maintain a low level of greenhouse gas emissions. National targets set by each country are to be regularly reviewed. The Climate Change Conference held in Bonn in 2017 addressed how to achieve this. The European Union (EU) spearheads international efforts for a global climate protection agreement. It strives to reduce emissions by at least 40 percent by 2030. The main tool is the EU emission trading scheme, which regulates the emission of carbon dioxide by around 11,000 major industrial corporations and power plant operators. It was reformed in 2018 with a view to making it more effective. Germany is also actively advancing climate cooperation with other countries and supports, for example, partner countries in achieving their national climate protection goals (Nationally Determined Contributions, NDCs) in the context of the NDC partnership established in 2016. These NDCs form the core of the Paris Agreement.

Germany's pioneering role in climate research is supported by work at universities and institutes such as the Potsdam Institute for Climate Impact Research and the Wuppertal Institute for Climate, Environment and Energy. ■

MILESTONES

1976

The then German Ministry of Research resolves to build a 100-metre-high large wind power plant (Growian) in north Germany. However, the first experiment with wind power fails and Growian is torn down in 1988.

1987

At Kaiser Wilhelm Koog on the west coast of Schleswig-Holstein, the first German windfarm goes turnkey. Since then, 32 wind turbines have been transforming North Sea wind into electrical power.

1991

The Electricity Feed-In Act regulates the obligation for power utilities to purchase electrical energy from regenerative transformation processes and sets fixed tariffs for the remuneration thereof.

The United Nations' Climate Secretariat in Bonn monitors the Framework Convention on Climate Change

2000

The Renewable Energy Sources Act (EEG) comes into force. Among other things, it lays the legal basis for prioritising renewable sources when feeding electricity into the national grid.

2011

After the nuclear reactor disaster in Fukushima the German Federal cabinet adopts parameters for energy policy: the exit from nuclear power is to be achieved step by step by 2022 and energy supplies placed on an eco-friendly footing.

2017

The German auto industry is increasingly investing in e-mobility. Some 40 billion euros will go into R&D by 2020. The number of electric models will treble from 30 to 100 over the same period.

TOPIC

ENERGY TRANSITION – A PROJECT FOR GENERATIONS

The Energy Transition is the single most important economic and environmental policy task in Germany. The Energy Transition refers to the restructuring of the country's energy supply sources away from fossil fuels and nuclear power, towards renewable energies. By 2050 at the latest, a minimum of 80 percent of electricity and 60 percent of all energy in Germany will come from renewable energies, so the plan. The next step will involve gradually shutting down all nuclear power stations by 2022. Since 2017 there have only been seven nuclear power stations still in operation, providing a good 10 percent of the electricity mix. The Federal Government is thus pressing ahead with the sustainable restructuring of the energy system, which began as long ago as 2000 with the first resolution on an exit from nuclear power and the promotion of the Renewable Energy Sources Act. In Germany the promotion of renewable energies began back in the 1990s and in the year 2000 was made into law in the form of the Renewable Energy Sources Act.

LIST

- Largest onshore wind farm: **Stössen-Teuchern in Saxony-Anhalt**
- Largest offshore wind farm: **alpha ventus in the North Sea**
- Most powerful wind turbine: **SG 8.0-167 DD by Siemens**
- Largest solar park: **Solarkomplex Senftenberg**
- Largest electricity exchange: **EEX (European Energy Exchange) in Leipzig**

Exit from nuclear power based on long-term planning

Likewise in the year 2000, the Federal Government agreed with the German energy companies on an exit from nuclear power by 2022. As such, the resolutions the Federal Government passed in 2011 follow in the tradition of restructuring of the energy system to rely on sustainable energy sources. It views the accelerated reorganisation of the energy system, which in 2011 the parties represented in the German Bundestag passed with the express approval of a large majority of the population following the nuclear disaster in Fukushima in Japan, as "a necessary step on the way to an industrial society committed to the idea of sustainability and the preservation of Creation".

However, it is not only the environment and climate that are intended to benefit from the Energy Transition, but the German economy as well – the primary aim being to

Offshore wind farms in the North Sea are the main pillars of the Energy Transition

eliminate reliance on international imports of crude oil and natural gas. To date, Germany spends around 45 billion euros annually on the import of coal, crude oil, and natural gas. In coming years, this amount will be gradually eliminated by domestic value added in the field of renewable energies; moreover, these measures result in additional export opportunities and the prospect of more jobs. Strengthening the "second pillar" of the Energy Transition – the more economical, more efficient use of energy – is another major task. Industry and large business enterprises have already achieved significant savings, and standards are high. Small companies and public facilities still have some catching up to do. Improving the energy consumption of old buildings in particular is especially important with regard to increasing energy efficiency, and the Federal ▸

Government makes grants available for the purpose. Buildings account for around 40 percent of carbon dioxide emissions. Electricity consumption also needs to be reduced: Further efforts are needed to reach the goal of a 10-percent reduction by 2020 outlined in the original energy concept.

The Energy Transition seeks not only to minimise risks, but also to enhance climate-compatible energy consumption and high supply security. The dynamic development of renewable energies has meant an increase in the proportion of carbon dioxide-free energy in the electricity mix. In 2017, green electricity had a 33.1-percent share. Depending on weather, at peak output solar and wind power plants can cover up to 90 percent of electricity demand in Germany.

Over 60 percent of all new residential buildings are already heated with renewable energies. In late 2017, there were 1.6 million solar PV systems installed, generating approx. 43 gigawatts in rated power, putting Germany in third place behind China and Japan in terms of nameplate capacity.

The Renewable Energy Sources Act an international benchmark

Regarded in several countries as a benchmark, the Renewable Energy Sources Act (EEG) was amended in 2014. The aim was to ensure that the population and business could afford energy, and that its supply was guaranteed. The background: As a result of the strong increase in the number of solar power systems and a different method of calculation, after 2009 there was a considerable increase in what is known as the EEG cost levy, whereby the increased cost of expanding green electricity is passed on to consumers on a pro-rated basis. This sparked a public debate on the cost of green electricity and the Energy Transition. A fall in this share in the costs was seen in 2015 for the first time. The Federal Government is also working on re-designing the structure of the electricity market to ensure stable supplies despite a

Electricity generation
In 2017 electricity generated from renewable energies increased yet again and accounted for 33.1 percent of gross electricity generation in Germany.

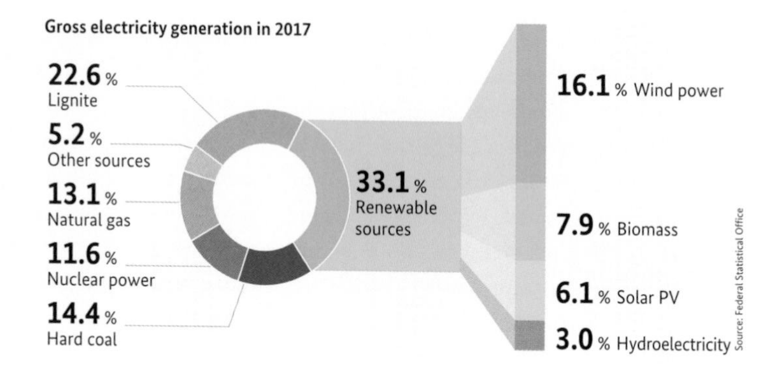

strong increase in the volume of fluctuating wind and solar power generated. Among other things it is about ensuring the availability of gas-fired power stations, which can be used as required, and which emit considerably less carbon dioxide than coal-fired power stations.

The Energy Transition requires not only the establishment of new, "green" power stations. To ensure a reliable supply, power grids have to be adapted to the new structure. To this end there are plans to add several hundred kilometres of "power highways". This way electricity from wind power, which is primarily generated in north Germany, can reach the strong economic hubs that are the centres of consumption in the south over long distances without major losses. The original plans to install overland cables were abandoned due to civil protests. In 2015 the Federal Government resolved to install underground cables. The major lines are now intended to go operational in 2025 at the earliest, and not 2022 as originally planned. In addition, the regional grids need to be expanded in order to be able to accommodate the solar power that is fed into the network from decentral sources. ■

GLOBAL

Climate study

800 scientists from 80 countries work for the United Nations' Intergovernmental Panel on Climate Change (IPCC).
In spring 2015, the panel of experts issued the Synthesis Report of the Fifth IPCC Assessment Report. It states that greenhouse gas emissions are the main cause of climate change. Drastic steps are needed if global warming is to be limited to two degrees Celsius.

→ ipcc.ch

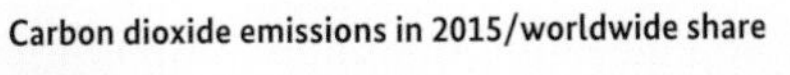

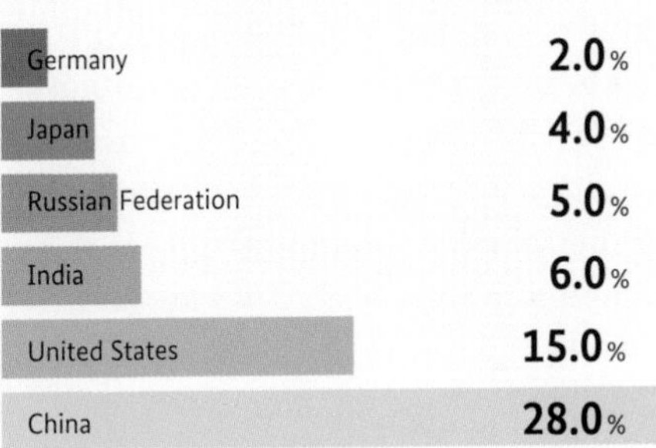

Share of electricity in Germany generated from renewable sources (terawatt forecast)

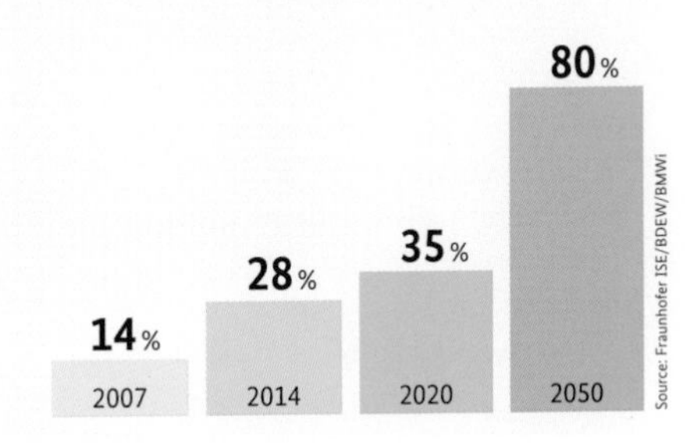

TOPIC

GREENTECH – A SECTOR WITH A FUTURE

Both the economy and the labour market are benefitting from the leading role Germany plays in technologies for environmental protection, renewable energies, and the efficient use of resources. The environment sector is making a considerable contribution to sustainable growth and is aiding the development of new technologies – in the fields of energy generation, ICT, and materials technology. Just under 700,000 people work in the energy sector; almost half of them in the field of renewable energies. This puts Germany among the six leading countries in terms of employment in this sector. Overall the latter is shaped by small to medium-size enterprises, though corporations such as Siemens are important players. Under the label "GreenTech Made in Germany" the companies are posting considerable export successes; their share of the global market is around 15 percent. With an "Environmental Technology Export Initiative" Germany intends to improve its situation still further and would like to position itself primarily as an integrated solutions provider.

Electromobility will be an important future issue in the environmental sector

Electromobility is also expected to give environmental and climate protection a further boost. The electromobility of the future is likewise a key issue being addressed today in China, Japan, and North America. The Federal Government and the automotive industry are jointly pursuing the ambitious goal of making Germany the leading market for electromobility and locking into the immense potential this global market has to offer. The plan is for the increasing number of electric cars to help lower carbon dioxide emissions still further, a sixth of which stems from road traffic. German car manufacturers are addressing e-mobility concepts in great depth. They are investing 40 billion euros in research and development by 2020 and aim to raise the number of models to over 100.

NUMBER

1.79 million

kilometres is the length of the German national grid. You could circumnavigate the globe at the Equator 45 times using the cables. The vast majority of the grid, namely a total of 1.44 million kilometres or 80 percent, is underground. Around 350,000 kilometres are power lines. The supra-regional high-voltage lines are 34,810 kilometres long. About 2,650 kilometres of new power lines are being planned as part of the Energy Transition.

→ **bundesnetzagentur.de**

Electromobility is one of the major topics the German automotive industry will address in the future

In order to help electric cars make their breakthrough, the Federal Government is supporting the development with buyer's premiums, tax incentives, and comprehensive subsidies to improve the charging infrastructure. It has also considerably increased spending on energy research, with a particular focus on more powerful batteries for electric cars. The "2020 Battery" project is regarded as a showcase project and is intended to produce evolutionary, advanced materials for R&D on the most efficient battery systems.

In the meantime German and European universities and higher education institutes now offer around 1,000 innovative courses in the field of renewable energies and energy efficiency, which attract many international students. ■

PANORAMA

SUSTAINABLE ENERGIES

Inner workings of a modern German wind turbine
Enercon E-126 type with a 4,200 kW power rating

1. Machine frame
2. Yaw drive
3. Ring generator
4. Blade pitch control
5. Rotor hub
6. Rotor blade

Wind power plants
The wind drives the rotor blades. The generator transforms the mechanical energy into electrical power.

Transformer house
The transformer feeds the power at the right voltage to the grid operator.

Substation
The substation transforms the medium voltage into high voltage for transmission over greater distances.

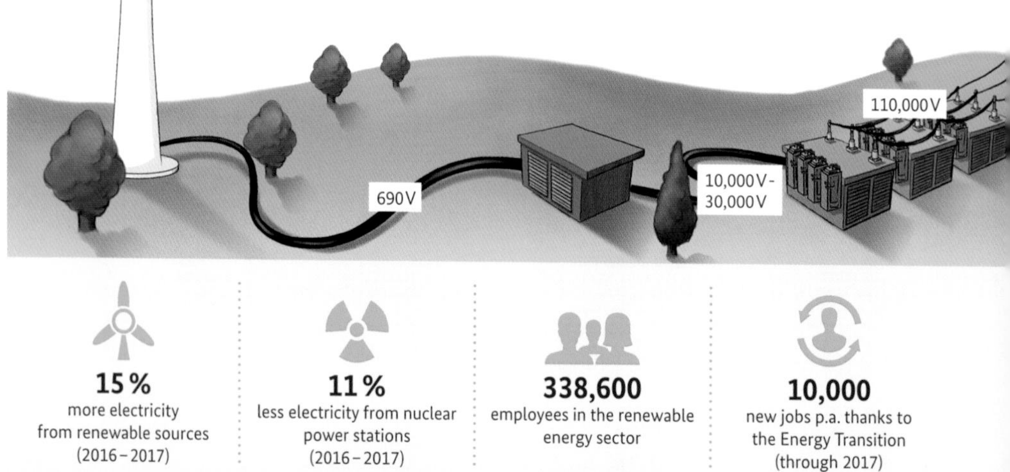

15 % more electricity from renewable sources (2016 – 2017)

11 % less electricity from nuclear power stations (2016 – 2017)

338,600 employees in the renewable energy sector

10,000 new jobs p.a. thanks to the Energy Transition (through 2017)

Use of wind power and solar energy by federal state
in output (MW)

- Solar energy
- Wind power

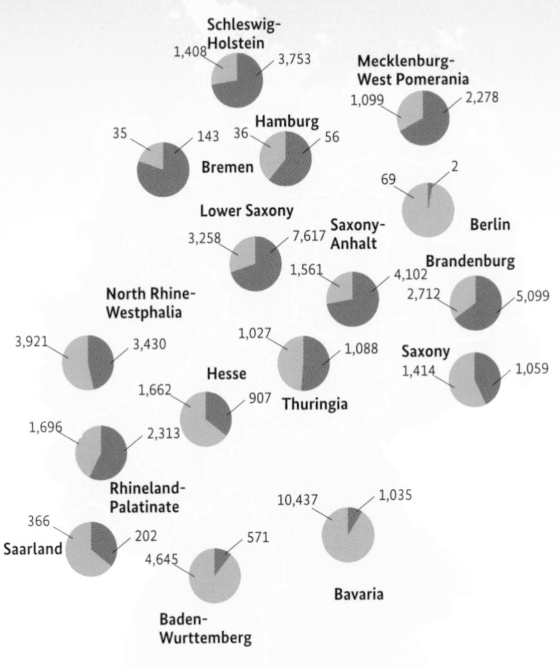

33.1 %

In 2017, 33.1 percent of the electrical energy consumed was generated by renewable sources.

28,675

In 2017 a total of 28,675 wind power plants were installed in Germany.

1.6 million

At year-end 2017 1.6 million solar PV plants were installed in Germany.

Power grid
Electricity is distributed to the individual regions via the high-voltage power grid.

Substation
In a second substation the high voltage is stepped down to 230 volts.

Households
A 5 MW wind power plant can supply electricity to some 4,900 households a year – and to about 14,600 persons.

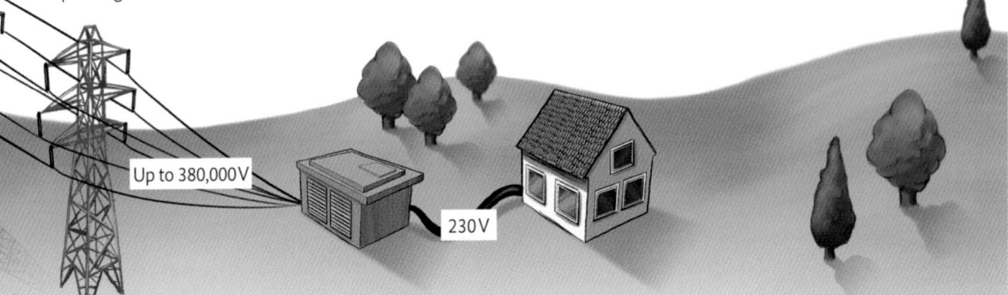

10.1 billion euros
for new wind power plants (2016)

1.5 billion euros
for new solar power plants (2016)

1.79
million kilometres of cable for the power grid

1,300
kilometres of “power highways”

TOPIC

ESSENTIAL DIVERSITY

Germany is a country with great biological diversity. Around 48,000 animal species, and 24,000 types of higher plants, mosses, fungi, lichens, and algae are native to the country. Having been enshrined in the Basic Law in 1994, the protection of the natural habitats is an official goal of government. Between the North Sea and the Alps, the lawmakers have designates 16 national parks and 16 UNESCO biosphere reserves that are totally different in character, along with thousands of nature reserves.

Germany is a signatory state to the most important international agreements on biodiversity, and a party to around 30 intergovernmental treaties and programmes with nature protection as their goal. By ratifying the United Nations' Convention on Biodiversity, the governments of 196 countries pledged to significantly reduce the rate of loss of biological diversity. To date, however, no turnaround in the extinction of species has been achieved. In 2010, an international framework for access to genetic resources and fair benefit sharing was passed at the Conference of Parties to the Convention in Nagoya (Japan). The Nagoya Protocol has been in force since 2014.

In Germany more than 40 percent of vertebrates and plant species are considered to be endangered. For this reason, efforts aimed at nature conservation and species protection on land, in the water, and in the North and Baltic Seas are to be stepped up. The primary objective is to reduce the destruction of habitats by house and road building, as well as the pollution levels that result, among other things, from intensive farming and over-fertilisation. The amount of land used for housing construction and new transport routes is intended to be reduced from 70 to 30 hectares daily. A further aim is to allow "wilderness" on two percent of the nation's territory and give five percent of forests over to nature. In 2015, numerous former military zones covering a total of 31,000 hectares, including moors and heaths, were devoted to nature conservation.

INFO

Wild animals For several years now, an increasing number of wild animals have been resettling in Germany. In more than 60 packs, an estimated total of up to 600 wolves are now roaming the eastern and northern federal states. Wild cats and lynxes are being sighted ever more frequently. The number of pairs of breeding sea eagles has reached unprecedented heights; otters are almost a familiar sight again. There have even been occasional sightings of elks and brown bears, which are wandering into Germany from neighbouring countries in the east.

→ **wwf.de**

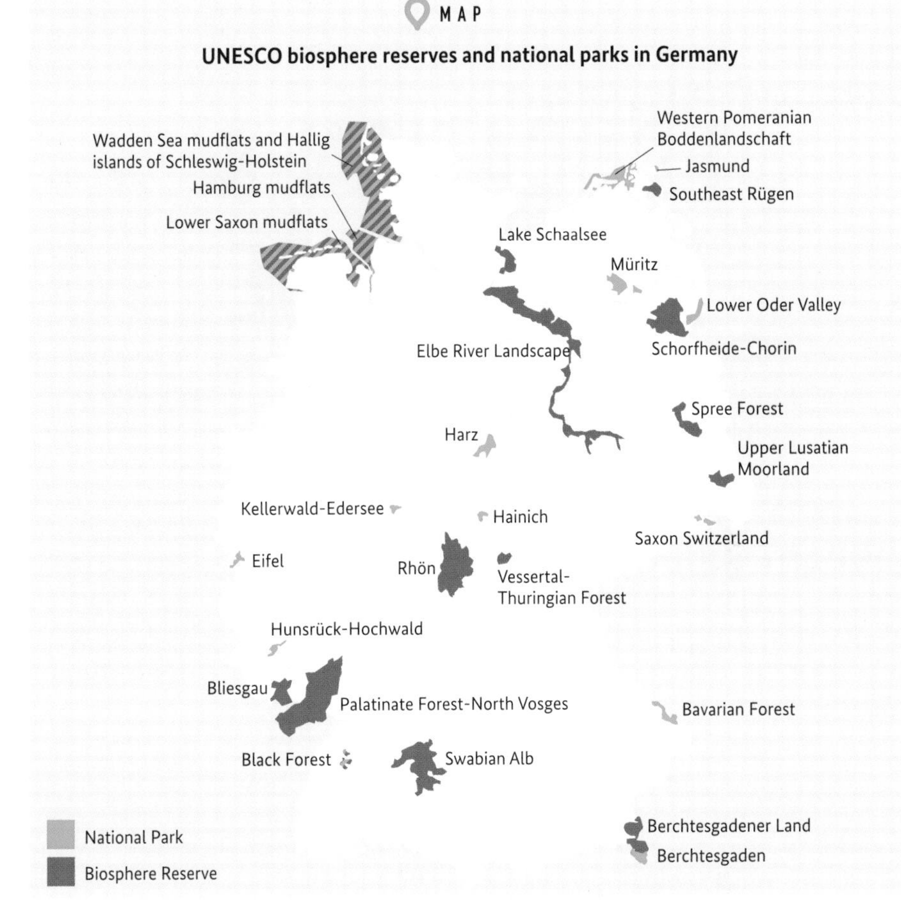

Increasing attention is being paid to protecting the marine environment. Seas are rich in biodiversity and a source of raw materials, energy, and food. Oil production, shipping, overfishing, littering with poorly degradable substances (plastic waste), and acidification caused by carbon dioxide put an immense strain on the ecosystem. In the context of Germany's G20 Presidency in 2017, government representatives and experts agreed on a joint action plan to stop the littering of the oceans. The Federal Government intends to use its EU Presidency in 2020 to ambitiously expand European environmental protection, with more funding for nature conservation and a new independent EU conservation fund. Particular attention will be given to the insect die-off. The Federal Government intends to launch an action plan to improve living conditions for insects. A scientific biodiversity monitoring centre is also to be established. ■

EDUCATION & KNOWLEDGE

Vibrant Hub of Knowledge • Dynamic Academic Landscape • Ambitious Cutting-edge Research • Networking Academia • Research and Academic Relations Policy • Excellent Research • Attractive School System

INSIGHT

VIBRANT HUB OF KNOWLEDGE

Germany is one of the top places in the world for research and academic training. This is symbolised by the fact that with more than 80 awards, Germany places third among the nations with the most Nobel laureates. In a globalised world in which knowledge is regarded as the most important resource, the country, with its long-standing tradition of research and development, is well positioned in the international competition for the best minds. Three major aspects shape this vibrant hub of knowledge: the dense network of around 400 higher education institutions, the four internationally renowned non-university research organisations, and strong industrial research. The country has its impressive research achievements to thank for the fact that within the European Union (EU) it is assured a firm place in the group of innovation leaders. Internationally, Germany is in the top group of those few countries to invest some 3 percent of their gross domestic product in research and development; the figure is set to be boosted to at least 3.5 percent by 2025.

With numerous measures and reforms, the government and higher education institutions took the initiative to advance Germany as a hub of knowledge and place it on a more international footing. The Qualification Initiative adopted in 2008 offers lifelong training programmes and forms part of this. Other success stories include the Excellence Initiative, which has spawned a number of internationally oriented graduate schools and clusters of excellence, a policy being continued by the Excellence strategy, the Higher Education Pact 2020, the High-Tech Strategy, the Research and Innovation Pact, and the Strategy for the Internationalisation of Science and Research. As Europe's biggest research nation, in 2014 Germany was the ▸

VIDEO AR APP

Education & Knowledge: the video on the topic → **tued.net/en/vid5**

As a place to study, Germany is one of the most popular destinations for international students

▸ first EU Member State to formulate a strategy for further shaping the European Research Area (ERA).

Particular attention is paid to an international focus. As part of the Bologna Process, most higher education courses now lead to Bachelor's and Master's degrees, with many of them offered in a foreign language. For international students Germany is one of the five most popular countries in which to study. At about 35 percent, the proportion of students from Germany who spend time studying abroad is high. The number of international members of staff at higher education institutions also rose steadily in recent years, and stands at over 10 percent. Many German higher education institutions are involved in the "export" of degree courses and the establishment of higher education institutions based on the German model in the international education market. In comparison with other countries, the German education system is in principle relatively well adapted to the needs of the labour market. 87 percent of adults in Germany have a university entrance qualification or successfully completed vocational training. The OECD average is only 86 percent. ■

→ INTERNET

Research Explorer
A research directory containing more than 25,500 institutes
→ **research-explorer.de**

Research in Germany
Major information platform about Germany as a centre of innovation
→ **research-in-germany.org**

DWIH
German Houses of Research and Innovation worldwide
→ **dwih-netzwerk.de**

Stepping-stone to a successful career: a university degree

COMPACT

PLAYERS & ORGANISATIONS

German Research Foundation

The German Research Foundation (DFG) is the main organisation for funding research at higher education and publicly financed institutes.

→ **dfg.de**

German Rectors' Conference

The German Rectors' Conference (HRK) is a voluntary association of state and state-recognised higher education institutions in Germany. The Higher Education Compass database provides information about degree courses and international cooperation agreements.

→ **hrk.de, hochschulkompass.de**

Leopoldina

The oldest academy of sciences in the world, the Leopoldina in Halle, has 1,500 members.

→ **leopoldina.org**

Non-university research organisations

The Max Planck Society, the Fraunhofer Gesellschaft, the Helmholtz Association, and the Leibniz Association are the non-university research organisations funded by the Federal Government and the states.

→ **mpg.de, fraunhofer.de, helmholtz.de, leibniz-gemeinschaft.de**

Alexander von Humboldt Foundation

The Humboldt Foundation supports cutting-edge scientists and scientific exchange.

→ **humboldt-foundation.de**

German Academic Exchange Service

The German Academic Exchange Service (DAAD) is the largest funding organisation for exchanges of students and academics. It has a global network with 71 regional offices and information centres.

→ **daad.de, studieren-in.de**

Alumniportal Deutschland

The Alumniportal Deutschland networks people who have studied, done research or worked in Germany all over the world.

→ **alumniportal-deutschland.org**

"Schools: Partners for the Future" initiative

The Federal Foreign Office initiative links almost 2,000 schools all over the world at which German is held in high esteem.

→ **pasch-net.de**

DIGITAL PLUS

More information about all the topics in the chapter – annotated link lists, articles, documents, speeches; plus more in-depth information about key topics such as the Bologna Process, internationalisation, degrees, admissions restriction.

→ **tued.net/en/dig5**

TOPIC

DYNAMIC ACADEMIC LANDSCAPE

The German academic landscape is highly diverse: There are famous universities in major cities such as Berlin and Munich, along with excellent higher education institutions in Aachen, Heidelberg, and Karlsruhe. Medium-sized universities with a strong focus on research and smaller colleges with an outstanding reputation form the nucleus of the academic world. Whether the international Shanghai Ranking, the QS World University Rankings, or the Times Higher Education World University Rankings – each lists between 12 and 20 German universities among the Top 200. Technical University of Munich, Munich's Ludwig-Maximilians-Universität and Heidelberg University do particularly well.

LIST

- Oldest university: **Heidelberg University (founded in 1386)**
- Youngest university: **Brandenburg Medical School (founded in 2014)**
- Biggest full university: **University of Cologne (53,176 students)**
- Most attractive university for international cutting-edge and young academics: **Freie Universität Berlin (2017 Humboldt Ranking)**

According to the German Rectors' Conference (HRK), in 2017 students in Germany could choose between 399 higher education institutions (120 universities, 221 universities of applied sciences, and 58 art and music academies). Together they offer 19,011 courses. As part of the Bologna Process to create a uniform European Higher Education Area (EHEA) initiated in 1999, almost all courses now lead to Bachelor's and Master's degrees. 240 higher education institutions are funded by the state, 39 by the church, and 120 privately.

Growing popularity among international students

In terms of structure and purpose, the higher education landscape is basically divided up threefold. We distinguish between universities, universities of applied sciences, and academies of art, film, and music. Whereas the classic universities offer a wide range of subjects, the technical universities (TU) concentrate on basic research in engineering and natural science disciplines. In 2006 the nine leading technical universities formed the TU9 Initiative. The universities regard themselves not only as teaching institutes but as research centres too, and as such even today embody Wilhelm von Humboldt's educational ideal of the unity of research and teaching. The universities' primary objective is to promote young academics, pass on substantiated specialist knowledge, and train academics to

There are 2.8 million students enrolled at around 400 higher education institutions in Germany

work and research independently. The 221 strongly practice-oriented universities of applied sciences (FH) are unique to Germany. The first introduction of the right of universities of applied sciences to award doctorates in the State of Hesse, which was previously only something universities were allowed to do, was a matter of much debate.

Overall, the number of people engaged in academic pursuits is increasing: Whereas in 2005 the ratio of freshmen stood at 37 percent, over half of young people in Germany now take up higher education. The Federal Training Assistance Act (BAföG) enables them to complete a degree course independently of their family's financial situation. Today, almost every second student comes from a non-academic home. In winter semester 2016-7 there were 2.8 million students registered at higher education institutions, among them 265,500 who gained their university ▸

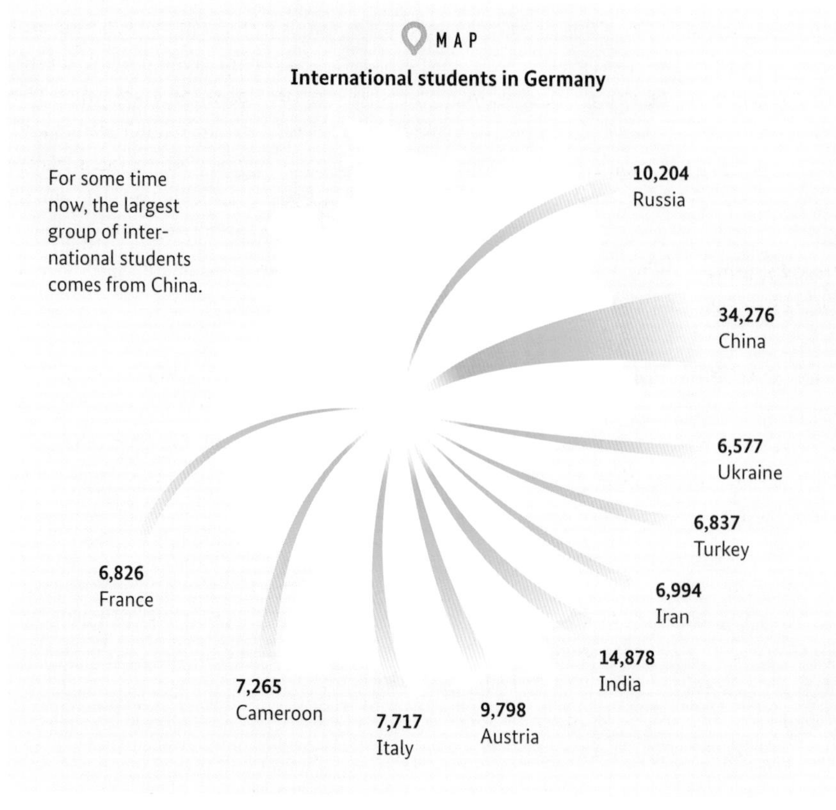

entrance qualification abroad – 41 percent more than in winter semester 2006-7.

Today there are more than twice as many foreigners enrolled at German universities as in 1996. Most international students come from China, India, and Russia. This puts Germany in the top five most most popular countries for international students.

At the same time the German higher education institutions have significantly increased the number of foreign-language and international courses: Around 1,400 courses are now taught in English. In over 730 courses, an international double degree is possible. The multitude of structured doctoral courses is particularly attractive for international doctoral students. The fact that for the most part most German higher education institutions do not charge tuition fees gives them a further advantage.

The Federal Government and the states are tackling the increasing numbers engaged in academic study together: In late 2014, as part of the Higher Education Pact 2020, they resolved to finance up to 760,000 additional university entrants in years thereafter. For the entire duration of the Higher Education Pact from 2007 to 2023, the Federal Government will provide 20.2 billion euros, and the states 18.3 billion euros.

Initiatives for more excellence and greater internationalisation

With the Excellence Initiative, between 2005 and 2017 the Federal Government and the states funded particularly outstanding research projects and facilities. In the second phase of the programme alone (2012–2017) total funding of 2.7 billion euros was provided to support 45 graduate schools, 43 clusters of excellence, and 11 institutional strategies spread across 39 universities. The subsequent Exellence strategy is initially not limited in time and will contribute 533 million euros a year from 2018 onwards. The strategy is intended to help German universities become even better on an international comparison. Promoting excellence clusters strengthens internationally competitive research areas in universities and university groups at the project level. If at least two excellence clusters are approved at one and the same university, the latter has a good chance of receiving permanent funding as a univesity of excellence.

Internationalisation remains an important topic. The German Rectors' Conference has identified more than 33,000 international cooperation agreements concluded with parner institutions in around 150 countries, among them many programmes leading to double degrees. Many higher education institutions are involved in the development of German study courses and the founding of higher education institutions based on the German model, which exist in Egypt, China, Jordan, Kazakhstan, Mongolia, Oman, Singapore, Hungary, Vietnam, and Turkey.

Increasing foreign mobility among German students is likewise being funded. Over one third already spend time studying abroad. In future it is intended that every second German graduate of a higher education institution gain experience abroad while studying. Scholarships such as the Erasmus+ programme support these valuable study visits. ■

INFO

Programme for Women Professors
Women in Germany are nowadays more likely than men to study, and write almost half of all doctoral theses – but less than one quarter of professors are female. This is why in 2008 the Federal Government and the states launched the Programme for Women Professors. With a budget of 200 million euros for the third phase from 2018-2022, the programme is designed to increase the number of women professors and promote equality. As part of the programme, over 500 woman professors have been appointed.
→ bmbf.de/de/494.php

TOPIC

AMBITIOUS CUTTING-EDGE RESEARCH

Science and research are held in high esteem in Germany. Over the past few years, businesses and the government have continually increased their knowledge work budgets. In 2016 the proportion of the gross domestic product (GDP) spent on research was 2.93 percent. Internationally this put Germany in the top group of countries that invest more than 2.5 percent of their GDP in research and development (R&D). In 2016 in Germany a total of almost 92.2 billion euros was spent on R&D. Industry sources just short of 63 billion euros of spending on research, with higher education institutions contributing about 16.5 billion and the state around 12 billion euros.

The European Commission's "European Innovation Scoreboard 2017" study places Germany, together with Sweden, Denmark, Finland, the Netherlands, and Great Britain in the top group of "innovation leaders" in the European Union (EU). The study emphasises that German industry's high investments in R&D are exemplary for Europe. Between 2006 and 2016, industrial companies in Germany increased spending on R&D to about 50 percent. Since 2005, joint R&D spending by government, industry, and higher education institutions has risen by 65 percent, and the plan is to boost the ratio of R&D spending to GDP to 3.5 percent by 2025.

German academics' results are highly presentable: In the Nature Index Global, which evaluates the publication output of research facilities and higher education institutions, published in 2018, Germany achieved top marks in Europe. At the international level it is in third place behind the USA and China.

DIAGRAM

Germany – a high-tech location
657,894 men and women work in research and development in Germany. Government spending on R&D rose in the 2005-17 period by over 90 percent. Germany is one of the world's top five in terms of investments in this segment.

Patents of relevance to global markets in EU countries, per million inhabitants

Sweden	435
Finland	423
Germany	372
Denmark	342
⋮	
EU average	154

Source: BMBF/Federal Report on Research and Innovation

Never before has investment in research and development been as high as it is today

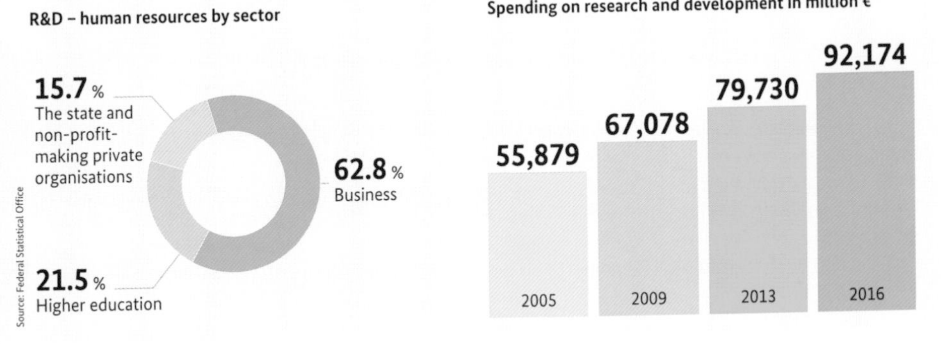

▸ **Since 2006 Germany** has developed a particular innovation tool in the form of its interdepartmental High-Tech Strategy. Since then, High-Tech Strategy research projects have prompted a raft of innovations – from energy-saving LED bulbs to a tissue-engineered heart valve. The High-Tech Strategy initially had the market potential of specific fields of technology in its sights, whereas since 2010 it has been focussing on society's need for solutions that are fit for the future, and their realisation.

As a research and innovation strategy, the High-Tech Strategy focuses on the major challenges of digitisation, health, climate and energy, mobility, security, social innovations, and the future of work. Within the framework of the High-Tech Strategy, 15 cutting-edge clusters which receive special funding were selected in three competition rounds. In 2014 an evaluation revealed that the cutting-edge clusters had produced 900 innovative products, 300 patents, 450 dissertation and habilitation theses, 1,000 Bachelor's and Master's theses, and 40 start-ups. Germany boasts around 1,000 publicly financed research facilities. Alongside higher education institutions, it is primarily four non-university research organisations that form the backbone of the research sector.

Excellent non-university research institutions

Founded in 1948, the Max Planck Society (MPG) is the most important centre for conducting basic research outside universities in the natural sciences, life sciences, social sciences, and the humanities. Over 14,000 researchers, 47 percent of them international scientists, work at the 84 Max Planck Institutes in Germany and research institutions, including six other institutes in the Netherlands, Luxembourg, Italy, the USA, and Brazil. Since it was established, the Max Planck Society has produced 18 Nobel laureates.

MILESTONES

1995
At the Fraunhofer Institute in Erlangen, a team headed by electrical engineer and mathematician Karlheinz Brandenburg develops the MP3 procedure for compressing audio data, which is nowadays standard throughout the world.

2005
The Excellence Initiative is announced for higher education institutions. The Joint Initiative for Research and Innovation provides funding for non-university research organisations.

2008
Nine years after the discovery of the giant magnetoresistance effect, which led to the breakthrough of gigabyte hard drives, the German Peter Grünberg and the Frenchman Albert Fert are awarded the Nobel Prize in Physics.

Since 1970 it has supported over 4,000 inventions through to market launch, and registers about 75 annually for patents.

The Helmholtz Association conducts cutting-edge research in six fields: energy, earth and environment, health, aeronautics, space and transport, key technologies and matter. The Helmholtz scientists concentrate on highly complex systems and projects. With just under 40,000 staff members at the 18 independent Helmholtz centres, including the German Aerospace Center (DLR), which has 20 sites in Germany alone, it is Germany's biggest research organisation.

With 72 institutes, the Fraunhofer-Gesellschaft is considered to be the largest application-oriented development organisation in Europe. Its most important fields of research are, for example, health and the environment, mobility and transportation, and energy and raw materials. With subsidiaries, branches and representative offices in no less than ten European countries, two in each of North and South America, seven Asian, two African countries, as well as in Israel, it has a truly global research reach.

The Leibniz Association is the umbrella connecting 93 independent research institutions that range in focus from the natural sciences, engineering, and environmental sciences through economics, spatial, and social sciences to the humanities. A focus common to the 9,900 researchers is knowledge transfer to policy makers, industry, and the general public.

The German Research Foundation (DFG), Europe's largest organisation of this kind, is responsible for funding science and research. Alongside its head office in Bonn, the DFG maintains offices in China, Japan, India, Russia, North and Latin America, and promotes cooperation between researchers in Germany and fellow researchers abroad. ■

2012

The European Patent Office honours Heidelberg physicist Josef Bille, the inventor of the eye laser, for his lifetime achievement. With almost 100 patents, Bille paved the way for present-day eye surgery using lasers.

2014

Stefan Hell, a Director at the Max Planck Institute for Biophysical Chemistry, together with two US researchers receives the Nobel Prize in Chemistry for developing high resolution fluorescence microscopy.

2017

Almost all courses have been switched over to Bachelor's and Master's degree courses. State-regulated degree courses, Medicine and Law are an exception.

TOPIC

NETWORKING ACADEMIA

Globalisation is also presenting the German academic landscape with new challenges. The ability to network knowledge and academics plays a major role here. In this respect, Germany has positioned itself well. Almost half of its academic publications are now written by researchers working on international co-operation projects. According to data compiled for the "Wissenschaft Weltoffen 2018" report, which provides facts and figures on the international nature of studies and research in Germany, there were 45,858 academic and artistic members of staff, among them 3,184 professors, working at 399 higher education institutions – that is almost 12 percent of all employees. Since 2010 the number of foreign academic staff has risen by more than one third. The recently simplified visa procedures for academics from non-EU member states has likewise played a role in promoting this development.

Asia, the Pacific Rim, and West Europe are the main areas of origin of the foreign academics receiving funding for a stay in Germany: Of late, each accounts for 18 percent of the total of 34,869 international experts recently supported. In many cases higher education institutions and research organisations set up welcome centres, so as to be able to give the international academics greater support as they settle in. Temporary stays by researchers are also regarded as beneficial, for having returned to their home countries, they often become important network partners for further collaborations.

Many academics from abroad are attracted to Germany by the country's excellent research infrastructure, which includes the opportunity to work on large-scale research facilities, which in some cases are the only ones of their kind in the world. The Helmholtz Association alone operates some 50 large-scale facilities for a wide range of research fields. Numerous academics from abroad, who are leading in their field, come to German universities on a Humboldt Professorship, Germany's most highly endowed research prize, which is worth five million euros and is awarded by the Humboldt Foundation.

14,359 German academics have received funding to conduct research abroad; the most important sponsors are the German Research Foundation (DFG), the European Marie Curie Fellowship programme, and in particular the German Academic Exchange Service (DAAD), the world's largest funding organisation for student and academic exchange, from which almost three quarters of the students and academics to receive funding were awarded a scholarship.

Germany aims to develop and expand international academic collaboration, while at the same time elevating it to the next level of quality. Amongst other things, the Federal

At German universities and academic institutes, research in international teams is part of everyday life

Government's new strategy to internationalise education, science, and research resolved in 2017 serves as the basis for this.

Ambitious realignment of the internationalisation strategy

The new internationalisation strategy responds to growing globalisation, digitisation, the advance of the European Research Area, and the emergence of new, global innovation centres outside established scientific hubs. The focus is on promoting international networking, world-wide cooperation in vocational training, partnerships with the Global South and emerging markets, and transnational efforts to overcome global challenges such as climate change, health, and food security. Strengthening the European Research Area plays a special role in strengthening Germany's position as a study and research space that is internationally attractive. ■

TOPIC

RESEARCH AND ACADEMIC RELATIONS POLICY

Academic exchange is a pillar of international cultural and educational policy. In its implementation, key partners of the Federal Foreign Office are the German Academic Exchange Service (DAAD), the Alexander von Humboldt Foundation, the German Archaeological Institute (DAI) along with the foundations of the political parties with an international focus. The Research and Academic Relations Initiative has since 2009 expanded its range of proven instruments and expanded them to include new strategies.

Thus, worldwide, five German Houses of Research and Innovation (DWIH) in Moscow, New Delhi, New York, São Paulo, and Tokyo promote scientific collaboration with Germany.

\# NUMBER

183.5 million

euros was the amount the Federal Foreign Office contributed to the budget of the German Academic Exchange Service (DAAD) in 2017. This is the biggest individual item, accounting for 34.8 percent in total. The funds are used to run a wide range of foreign cultural and education policy projects and programmes.

Furthermore, since 2009 the German Academic Exchange Service has funded the work of four new Centres of Excellence in Russia, Thailand, Chile, and Colombia: these network hundreds of international scientists with German research and train young academics to the highest standards. In Subsaharan Africa since 2008 ten expert centres have also been established that symbolise new research capacities and an improved quality of education.

Academic cooperation with crisis and conflict regions

A major focal point of the German foreign cultural and education policy in times of crisis and in regions in conflict as well as in transition countries is to enable access to education and research and thus create scientific and academic prospects. With this complex commitment there are hopes that cooperation in research and higher education can pave the way for political understanding, and that as such crisis prevention and crisis management can frequently be made possible.

Strengthening academic freedom

The numerous crises and conflicts the world has seen in the most recent past result in young people being denied education and academic freedom coming under ever greater pressure. In response to this, the Federal For-

Federal Foreign Minister Maas (in the centre) with alumni of the DAAD "Managers for Syria" Programme

eign Office funds the Alexander von Humboldt Foundation's Philipp Schwartz Initiative, which enables threatened researchers to work in Germany. And the German Academic Exchange Service in 2014 teamed up with the Federal Foreign Office to launch the "Leadership for Syria" programme, which ensured 221 Syrian scholarship holders could study in Germany and graduate. Moreover, the Federal Foreign Office promotes Sur-Place scholarship programmes for refugees in first host countries. Particularly worthy of mention in this context is the Albert Einstein German Academic Refugee Initiative (DAFI), which is run by the Federal Foreign Office together with the United Nations High Commission for Refugees (UNHCR); there are also additional Sur-Place scholarships available through the DAAD.

German educational and academic institutions thus create prospects and keep access open where university and research policy conditions are otherwise tough. The DAAD has also teamed up with the German Federal Ministry of Education and Research to launch the "Integra – Integration of Refugees into Vocational Studies" and "Welcome – Students Support Refugees" programmes.

Since 2001 Germany has conducted a transformation partnership with several Arab countries. The idea is to support reform efforts at Arab universities through cooperation projects with German higher education institutions. Moreover, the numerous "Good Governance" programmes aimed at future leaders in crisis regions worldwide constitute a particularly important field. ■

PANORAMA

EXCELLENT RESEARCH

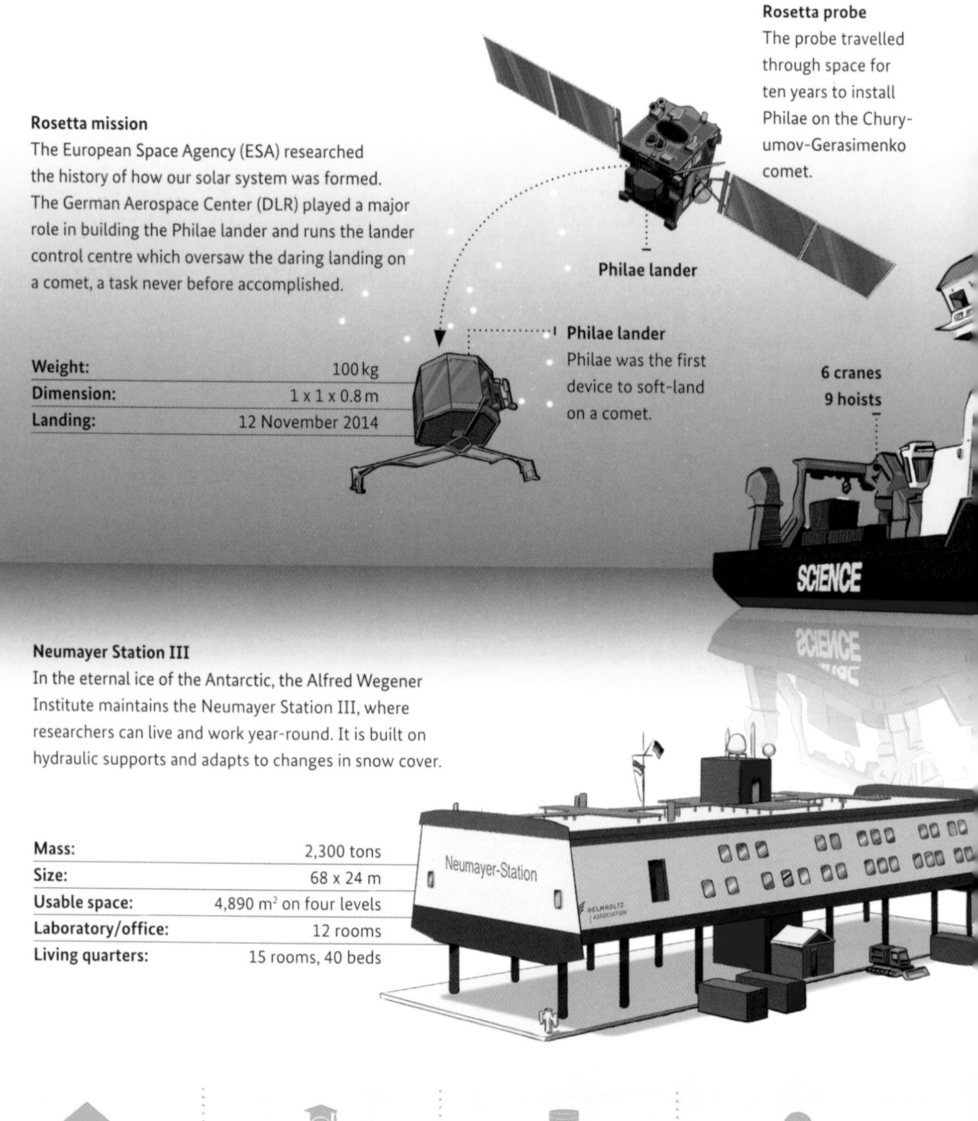

Rosetta probe
The probe travelled through space for ten years to install Philae on the Chury-umov-Gerasimenko comet.

Rosetta mission
The European Space Agency (ESA) researched the history of how our solar system was formed. The German Aerospace Center (DLR) played a major role in building the Philae lander and runs the lander control centre which oversaw the daring landing on a comet, a task never before accomplished.

Weight:	100 kg
Dimension:	1 x 1 x 0.8 m
Landing:	12 November 2014

Philae lander
Philae was the first device to soft-land on a comet.

Neumayer Station III
In the eternal ice of the Antarctic, the Alfred Wegener Institute maintains the Neumayer Station III, where researchers can live and work year-round. It is built on hydraulic supports and adapts to changes in snow cover.

Mass:	2,300 tons
Size:	68 x 24 m
Usable space:	4,890 m² on four levels
Laboratory/office:	12 rooms
Living quarters:	15 rooms, 40 beds

399
higher education institutes and universities

2.8 million
students at higher education institutions

€ 92.2 billion
spent on research and development

586,030
researchers

Sonne research vessel

Sonne is the most recent addition to the German research fleet and has been probing the secrets of the deep sea since 2014, primarily in the Pacific and in the Indian Ocean. The high-tech ship is regarded as one of the most modern in the world.

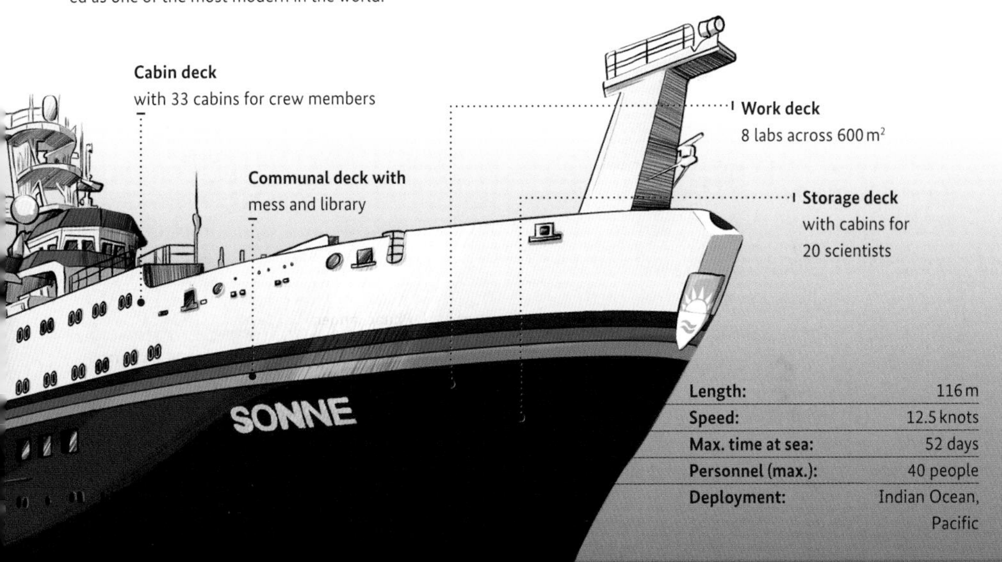

Length:	116 m
Speed:	12.5 knots
Max. time at sea:	52 days
Personnel (max.):	40 people
Deployment:	Indian Ocean, Pacific

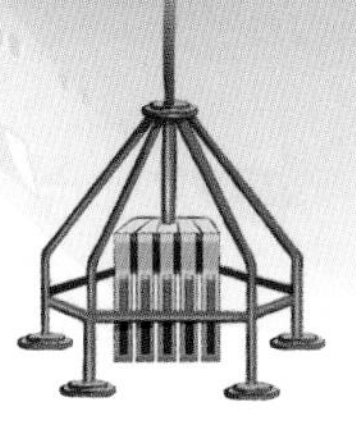

Multi-corer
It can simultaneously take lots of small samples from the seabed.

Water extractor
This device takes water samples and measures temperature and depth.

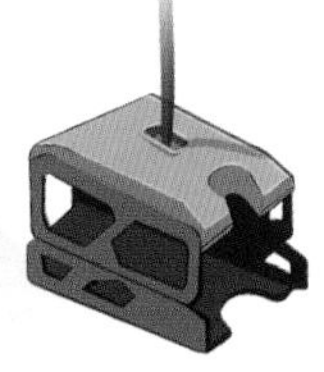

Underwater vehicle
It is remote controlled and equipped with a video camera and gripper arms.

81
Max Planck Institutes worldwide

72
Fraunhofer Institutes

93
Leibniz Association research facilities

18
Helmholtz Association research centres

TOPIC

ATTRACTIVE SCHOOL SYSTEM

In Germany responsibility for the school system is primarily with the 16 federal states. This is why there are different education systems and plans, along with different types of school. The Standing Conference of the Ministers of Education and Cultural Affairs of the Länder in the Federal Republic of Germany (KMK) guarantees the conformity or comparability of the education programmes and the certificates awarded. In the 2016-7 academic year there were almost 11 million pupils attending 42,322 generaleducation and vocational schools, with 798,180 teachers giving instruction. Furthermore there are some 990,402 pupils enrolled at 5,836 private general-education and vocational schools. In general, school attendance is compulsory for all children from the age of six for a nine-year period. At the same time the promotion of early education at pre-school age and its interlocking with primary schooling is a high-priority issue in education policy. About 20,000 all-day schools now have a firm place in the education system. It is expected that teaching in these schools will spell an increased level of equal opportunities specifically for children from educationally deprived backgrounds.

GLOBAL

PISA survey Published in early 2018, the special evaluation of the Programme for International Student Assessment (PISA) comparative survey conducted by the OECD revealed that the differences in achievements between socially better-off schoolchildren and those from socially disadvantaged families remains pronounced, as does the statistical link between achievements and social roots. However, the trend is positive. In Germany, equal opportunities have increased in this regard.
→ **oecd.org/pisa**

Attendance at state schools is free of charge. The school system is divided vertically into three levels: primary education and secondary education levels I and II. As a rule, all children attend a primary school, which lasts from Year 1 to 4 (in Berlin and Brandenburg 1 to 6). Subsequently there are three standard curricula: the secondary general school curriculum (Years 5 to 9 or 10), the intermediate school curriculum (Years 5 to 10, "Mittlere Reife" or middle school diploma) and the grammar school curriculum (Years 5 to 12 or 13, general higher education entrance diploma; or Abitur). These are taught either in separate types of school or in schools which combine two or – as in the case of comprehensive schools – three of the curricula and facilitate switching between the different types of school. The names of these types of school vary depending on the state; only grammar schools (Gymnasium) are known as such in

Some 9 million pupils attend general-education schools

all states. In 2017 about 440,000 pupils were awarded the higher education entrance diploma entitling them to study at a university or university of applied sciences. For children with special needs there are separate schools which, depending on the particular disability, provide adequate facilities to help them learn and develop. In line with the UN Convention on the Rights of People with Disabilities, children with and without disabilities being taught together is intended to become the rule.

In 72 countries the 140 German schools abroad provide an excellent education to around 22,000 German and 60,000 non-German pupils. Most are run privately, but are supported by the Central Agency for German Schools Abroad (ZfA). Since 2008 the PASCH initiative, ZfA, and Goethe-Institut have been working on forming an even bigger network of German students. Worldwide it links almost 2,000 schools, with more than 500,000 pupils learning German there. ■

SOCIETY

Enriching Diversity • Structuring Immigration •
Diverse Living Arrangements • Committed Civil Society • Strong Welfare State •
Leisure Time and Travel • Freedom of Religious Worship

INSIGHT

ENRICHING DIVERSITY

With some 82.6 million inhabitants, Germany is the most populous nation in the European Union. The modern, cosmopolitan country has developed into an important immigration country. A good 18.6 million people in Germany have a migratory background. Germany is now among those nations with the most liberal immigration rules. According to a 2017 study by the Organisation for Economic Co-operation and Development (OECD), it is the most popular immigration country after the USA.

Most people in Germany have a high standard of living, on an international comparison, and the corresponding freedom to shape their own lives. The United Nations' Human Development Index (HDI) 2016 ranks Germany fourth of 188 countries. In the Nation Brands Index 2017, an international survey on the image of 50 countries, Germany tops the scale – also owing to its high values in the areas of quality of life and social justice. Germany considers itself a welfare state, whose primary task is to protect all its citizens.

German society is shaped by a pluralism of lifestyles and ethno-cultural diversity. New ways of life and everyday realities are changing daily life in society. Immigrants enrich the country with new perspectives and experiences. There is great social openness and acceptance as regards alternative ways of life and different sexual orientations. Advances are being made in terms of gender equality and traditional gender role assignments are no longer rigid. People with disabilities are taking an ever greater role in social life.

▸

VIDEO AR APP

Society: the video on the topic
→ **tued.net/en/vid6**

A high standard of living and great individual freedom shape quality of life in Germany

▸ **In future, demographic** change is set to shape Germany more than virtually any other development. The birth rate has recently edged up, but is still a comparatively modest 1.5 children per woman. Life expectancy is at the same time rising. By 2060 the population in Germany is estimated to shrink – depending on the scale of immigration to as low as 67.6 million according to the German Federal Statistical Office. At the same time, the growing number of elderly people is presenting social welfare systems with new challenges.

Socioeconomic change in Germany in recent years has led to the emergence of new social risks and stronger social diversification according to economic living conditions. Although in 2017 unemployment was at the same low level as in 1991 (on average 2.5 million), almost one in five in Germany is at risk of poverty, particularly young people and single parents. Moreover, social differences continue to exist between east and west. ■

→ INTERNET

Deutsch plus
Interdisciplinary network and initiative for a pluralist republic
→ **deutsch-plus.de**

Make it in Germany
Multilingual welcome portal for international skilled workers
→ **make-it-in-germany.com**

Human Development Reports
Where does Germany stand on a global comparison?
→ **hdr.undp.org**

Demographic change is presenting the nation with major challenges

COMPACT

PLAYERS & ORGANISATIONS

Federal Office for Migration and Refugees
The Federal Office offers complete information on residence in Germany and makes decisions relating to applications for asylum.
→ **bamf.de**

German Islam Conference
Since 2006 a long-term dialogue between the German state and Muslims living in Germany has been in place in the form of the German Islam Conference (DIK).
→ **deutsche-islam-konferenz.de**

Federal Volunteer Service
The service is geared towards women and men who want to get involved in working for the common good – in a social, ecological, or cultural context or in sport, integration, or civil protection and disaster response.
→ **bundesfreiwilligendienst.de**

National Action Plan for Integration
Germany seeks to achieve a high level of integration, which is why the topic has been a focal point of the Federal Government's work since 2005. An integration summit takes place annually.
→ **bundesregierung.de**

Polling institutes
Several established opinion polling institutes regularly survey Germans' opinions and publish projections on election days. Among the best known are Forschungsgruppe Wahlen, Forsa, Emnid, Infratest Dimap, and Institut für Demoskopie Allensbach.

Federal Employment Agency
The national employment agency is responsible for job placement and employment promotion as well as financial compensation.
→ **arbeitsagentur.de**

Foundations
Germany has one of the highest densities of foundations in Europe. On a national average, there are 26.5 foundations for every 100,000 inhabitants. The best known is Stiftung Warentest, which tests and compares products on behalf of the government.
→ **stiftungen.org**

DIGITAL PLUS
More information on all topics in this chapter – link lists with additional comments, articles, documents; plus more detailed information on terms such as demographic change, social security, intergenerational contract, equal rights, and standard of living.
→ **tued.net/en/dig6**

TOPIC

STRUCTURING IMMIGRATION

Germany has emerged as one of the world's most preferred destinations for migrants. The Organisation for Economic Cooperation and Development (OECD) stated in 2017 that Germany remains no. 2 only to the USA as the most popular country for immigration. In none of the 35 OECD member states has migration risen as fast in recent years as in Germany. In 2015 the figure of two million new foreigners set a record. Many of them came seeking protection, above all wars and conflicts, e.g., in Syria and Iraq, led to many people fleeing their home countries and seeking shelter elsewhere. In 2016 the figure had dropped to about 1.7 million migrants, and has continued to fall since.

The Federal Government champions reducing the causes of flight and irregular migration as well as actively structuring and controlling migration processes. This includes people with no prospect of residence in Germany returning to their countries of origin, and support for their reintegration there. In 2016 there were a total of some 10 million foreign passport holders living in Germany. 18.6 million persons had a migrant background, including immigrants, foreigners born in Germany, and persons who had a parent who was either an immigrant or a foreigner. The group thus accounts for over 22 percent of the total population. 9.6 million persons with a migrant background were German passport holders; of them, 42 percent have been German citizens since birth. A further 33 percent themselves immigrated to Germany as (late) repatriates; the remaining 25 percent have taken German citizenship. In 2016 alone almost 110,400 foreigners acquired German citizenship.

DIAGRAM

Modern immigration society
Germany is the second-most popular destination for immigrants in the world after the United States. In 2016 altogether some 18.6 million people in Germany had a migratory background. There are around four to five million Muslims living in Germany – only roughly half of them consider themselves religious, equating to 2.5 to 3 percent of the population.

Population according to migration status 2016

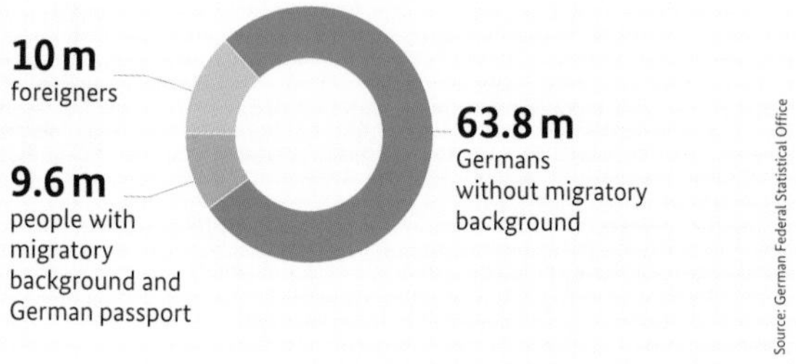

In Germany 18.6 million people have a migratory background

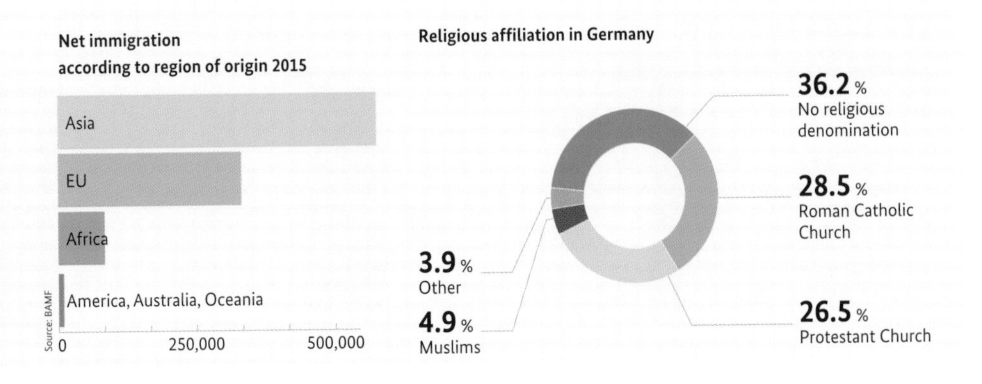

▸ **Migrants play a key role** in Germany's social and economic development. The growing need for skilled workers has brought increasingly well qualified migrants to Germany and the Federal Government wishes to enable further immigration amongst others to counteract the lack of skilled labour resulting from demographic change. Flanking greater activation of the in-country pool for potential employment and of immigration from EU member states, the Federal Government also considers immigration by skilled labour from third-party countries a way to blunt the impact of demographic change and help secure the base of skilled labour.

Highly qualified migrants are granted an EU Blue Card, facilitating their entry into the German labour market. Skilled labour from non-EU countries with recognised vocational training in certain bottleneck fields, such as the health and care professions, can come to Germany to work. To exhaust the potential in full, legislation is planned to interface the regulations on immigration.

Integration as a key element of migration policy

Integration policy is a core policy area in Germany and is considered a task for all of society. Integration is a service, but also requires migrants to commit to making efforts themselves as it can only succeed as a mutual process. According to the Residency Act, those foreigners who legally live long-term on German territory can lay claim to federal integration services. These services include language instruction, integration in training, work, and education, as well as social integration. The goal: to enable such persons to be part of and play a part in society. The central measure: an integration course consisting of language instruction and an orientation course.

More than 30 percent of the 20-34 year-old foreign adults remain without vocational qualifications. A key goal of the Federal Government: to enhance their participation in education. The reform of the citizenship laws

MILESTONES

1955
Strong economic growth leads to a shortage of labour in Germany in the mid-1950s. Recruitment agreements with Italy, Spain, Greece, Turkey, Morocco, Portugal, Tunisia, and Yugoslavia follow.

1964
The millionth migrant worker, called "Gastarbeiter", is welcomed to Germany. Recruitment is halted in 1973 with the oil crisis. Now around four million foreigners are living in Germany.

1990
Immigration increases rapidly in 1990 with the fall of the Iron Curtain and the wars in former Yugoslavia. Moreover, 400,000 people of German origin arrive in Germany from Central and Eastern Europe.

in 2014 introduced dual citizenship. For persons who were born and have grown up in Germany after 1990 and are the children of foreign parents, the "obligation" to opt for either the one or the other citizenship after completing their 23rd year has been abolished.

Protection for refugees and the politically persecuted

The Basic Law guarantees politically persecuted persons a right to asylum. In this way, Germany affirms its historical and humanitarian responsibility. In 2015 – as part of the so-called "refugee crisis", 890,000 arrived in Germany seeking protection, and in 2016 about 746,000 persons applied for asylum. The number of persons seeking protection in Germany has since been falling, with some 223,000 applications for asylum filed in 2017, with the figure approx. 64,000 for January-April 2018. Germany advocates a European solution to the refugee issue based on solidarity. The Federal Government is at the same time committed to improving refugee protection and supporting refugees in their host countries. ■

GLOBAL

OECD study on the integration of immigrants In recent years Germany has succeeded in integrating immigrants ever better in the labour market. Yet deficits are still evident among children of parents born abroad. These are the findings of a comparative study by the Organisation for Economic Co-operation and Development (OECD) entitled "Indicators of Immigrant Integration 2015".
→ **oecd.org**

1997
Alongside migrant workers, since the mid-1980s ever more asylum seekers have been coming to Germany. From 1997 the Dublin Convention determines responsibilities of the EU states regarding asylum procedures.

2005
The "Microcensus" offers the very first opportunity to survey the migratory background of the population. According to the census, in 2015 every fifth person in Germany has a migrant background.

2014
More than 200,000 people apply for asylum in Germany in 2014. For the first time, almost half a million more people move to Germany than leave it in the same period.

TOPIC

DIVERSE LIVING ARRANGEMENTS

Even in the individualised and highly mobile world of the 21st century, family is accorded a central role. For almost eight out of ten Germans, family continues to be the most important social institution and influential reference group. At the same time ideas about the typical family form are changing. Less than half the people in Germany live in a family unit. Despite the decline of traditional family structures, in 2016 married couples with children under 18 constituted the most common family form at almost 70 percent. The number of marriages has recently edged up; in 2016 the figure was 410,000. A little more than one in three marriages ends in divorce. The average length of marriages that ended in divorce in 2016 was 15 years. Around 46,000 marriages took place between Germans and foreigners in 2015.

The number of unmarried couples with children living together is significantly increasing. Between 1996 and 2013 the figure doubled to 11.6 million families today; almost every tenth couple with a child is unmarried. Families with just one parent are also a growing family form. Today single parents make up a fifth of all parent-child constellations and almost nine out of ten of the 2.7 million single parents are women. Single parents are often at considerable risk of enduring poverty; more than half draw state benefits.

Same-sex partnerships are among those forms of living that are gaining in significance. In 2015 there were 94,000 homosexual couples living together in Germany – over 50 percent more than ten years before. Around 43,000 of them live in a registered partnership, which has since 2001 ensured that same-sex couples' relationships are legally recognised. In 2017, the Bundestag enacted the so-called "Marriage for all". Homosexual couples now have the right to a full marriage and thus, for example, also to adopt children.

Whereas on the one hand new forms of cohabitation are emerging, on the other the number of one-person households is on the rise. 41 percent of all private households are single households. While this development is a result of demographic change, with the number of elderly people living alone increasing, more young people are also living alone.

Targeted support for families with parental leave and family allowance

Structures are likewise changing within families. Intergenerational relationships between parents and children are often good and as a rule are not characterised by traditional or authoritarian upbringing patterns, but by involvement, affection, encouragement, and the promotion of independence.

Great importance is attached to family – a great many fathers now also take parental leave

The proportion of working mothers has risen to over 66 percent (2006: 61 percent). More than 70 percent of working women with children work on a part-time basis however, especially those whose children are not yet at school; the corresponding figure for working fathers is just five percent. In 2014 the employment rate of women in Germany was 74 percent, clearly above the EU average (68.5 percent).

The parental leave introduced in 2007 enables more easily to reconcile starting a family with professional further development. Parental leave gives both partners the option of suspending their job for up to three years. During this period they receive family allowance for up to 14 months amounting to 67 percent of their last net income (minimum of 300, maximum of 1,800 euros) to secure their livelihood. ▸

New forms of cohabitation, such as in same-sex partnerships, are accepted

▸ **75 percent of** Germans consider family allowance to be a good arrangement; almost all parents take advantage of the benefit. However, four out of five fathers only take the minimum period of two months off. It continues to be primarily mothers who stay at home for a longer period after having children. The Elterngeld Plus family allowance scheme launched in 2015 makes returning to work early on even more worthwhile: Parents who work part-time receive financial support for up to 28 months.

The number of nursery places for under-threes has more than doubled

Since 1 August 2013 children have had a legal right to a nursery place upon reaching the age of one. Today every third child under three (763,000 children in 2017) attends one of the 55,000 day-care facilities or is cared for by one of 44,000 child minders. The number of nursery places for under-threes has more than doubled since 2006.

Parental leave, family allowance, and improved overall conditions for day-care for babies and pre-schoolers continue to create the preconditions for the equal treatment of women as laid down in the Basic Law. Whereas in the education sector young women have not only caught up with, but in part overtaken young men (in 2017 53.1 percent of those who attained a university entrance qualification were women, 50.5 percent of new students in 2016 were women), there are still differences between the sexes as regards pay and career paths: On average women working full-time only earn around 79 percent of the salary of their male counterparts. They also continue to be underrepresented in managerial roles. Today, about every seventh board member of DAX corporations is a woman.

In 2015 the Law on Equal Participation of Women and Men in Leadership Positions entered into force in the private and public sector. Among other things, it stipulates that women must occupy 30 percent of seats on the supervisory councils of companies listed on the stock exchange. Moreover, in its Coalition Agreement in 2018 the Federal Government set the target of equal gender participation in managerial functions in the civil service by 2025. Of late, the proportion of women in the Bundestag has fallen: It is currently at 30.9 percent. That said, until 1983 less than 10 percent of the parliamentarians were women.

Inclusion as an important social responsibility

The Federal Government also aims to create equal opportunities for people with disabilities. It is working towards an inclusive society in which everyone can participate equally: at school, at work, in leisure time. This requires comprehensive accessibility – and the aim is to remove both obstacles in buildings, on streets and paths and social hurdles, such as access to the labour market.

In 2007 Germany was one of the first states to sign the United Nations Convention on the Rights of Persons with Disabilities, with a national action plan structuring its implementation. Among other things, it envisages intensive preparation measures for working life for severely disabled youths. Going beyond the action plan, a federal participation law was enacted in 2017.

The elderly constitute a further group whose needs and potential the Federal Government particularly has in mind. More than every fifth person in Germany is aged 65 years or older. Their wealth of experience is considered beneficial to society. Their ways of life have likewise diversified and changed; overall elderly people are considerably more active today than in the past. They are frequently also still integrated in the labour market. As meeting places, 540 multigenerational houses promote an intensive dialogue between old and young, bringing together people of different ages. ■

INFO

Shell Youth Study What makes young people in Germany "tick"? What is important to them, how do they spend their spare time, what is their relationship like to their parents and friends? Since 1953 the oil-and-gas company Shell has regularly commissioned independent research institutes to paint a portrait of young people. The 17th Shell Youth Study was published in 2015.
→ shell.de/aboutshell/our-commitment/shell-youth-study.html

TOPIC

COMMITTED CIVIL SOCIETY

Around 31 million Germans are involved in voluntary work in their spare time, thus assuming responsibility for society. This commitment is often long term – one third of volunteers has been active for ten years. Almost 60 percent of those polled in the Federal Government's 14th Volunteers Survey spend up to two hours a week on voluntary work. Together with charities, churches, cooperatives, aid organisations, non-profit organisations, and private initiatives, the members of more than 600,000 associations form the backbone of this "third sector". Civil society refers to the section of society that is not shaped by government or party politics, but gets involved in social and political issues voluntarily and publicly.

Foundations in particular have become increasingly significant. With more than 21,000 incorporated foundations under civil law, the classic legal form of a foundation, Germany has one of the highest numbers of foundations in Europe. Since the turn of the millennium some 13,500 civil-law foundations have been established; more than half of all foundations of this kind in existence today. On a national average, there are 26.5 foundations for every 100,000 inhabitants. Taken together, all foundations have assets amounting to approximately 68 billion euros. They spend around 4.3 billion on charitable causes, traditionally social issues, education, science, and culture. The five largest foundations under private law in terms of expenditure are the Volkswagen Foundation, Robert Bosch Stiftung, Bertelsmann Stiftung, Hans Böckler Foundation, and WWF Deutschland.

Community foundations are strongly on the rise, foundations in which several citizens and firms act as joint funders to support local or regional projects. The first foundations of this kind were established in 1996 – in mid-2016 there were already more than 300 community foundations recognised by the Association of German Foundations. Civil commitment has slightly increased in recent years, but is shifting more strongly away from the larger associations and towards small, self-organised groups and alternating projects. Currently there are numerous people in Germany involved on a voluntary basis in local initiatives supporting refugees.

Involvement in parties, trade unions, and non-governmental organisations

Socio-political involvement in parties, trade unions, and NGOs enables people to help shape things on a strategic and political level. Here volunteering opens a door to intensive democratic participation. The major established organisations however are finding it increasingly difficult to get volunteers on board.

Environmental protection is an issue many people actively work for in their spare time

There is particular potential for volunteer work in the 14 to 24-year age bracket. The interest in volunteer services shows that young adults are willing to get involved in society. The Federal Volunteer Service has been in place since 2011. It is open to all age groups and complements the model, in existence for over 50 years, of the voluntary social year for young people and young adults. In early 2018, more than 43,000 such volunteers were serving. It is also possible to do voluntary work abroad, for example through the International Volunteer Service of the Federal Ministry for Family Affairs, Senior Citizens, Women and Youth, the Weltwärts programme of the Federal Ministry for Economic Cooperation and Development, or the Kulturweit volunteer service by the German UNESCO Commission in cooperation with the German Federal Foreign Office. ■

TOPIC

STRONG WELFARE STATE

Germany has one of the most comprehensive welfare systems. As in other developed democracies, in Germany too social spending represents the largest individual item of public spending. Around 918 billion euros was committed to public social spending in 2016, equating to a share of 29 percent of gross domestic product (GDP). The tradition of the state welfare system goes back to the age of industrialisation in Germany in the second half of the 19th century and is associated with then Reich Chancellor Otto von Bismarck. It was under Bismarck that firstly mandatory health insurance for workers was introduced in 1883, and with the social legislation that was expanded in the following years the basis was created for an orientation on the welfare state. The principle of the welfare state is embedded in article 20, paragraph 1 and article 28 of the Basic Law of the Federal Republic of Germany. Politicians and social players must continually renegotiate which form it takes in a dynamic process; particularly demographic change necessitates adjustments.

#NUMBER

32.6 m

is the number of employees subject to mandatory social insurance contributions that the Federal Employment Agency counted in December 2017. This equates to 75 to 80 percent of all employees. The figure does not include those not subject to mandatory social insurance contributions, i.e. civil servants, the self-employed, unpaid family workers, and mini-jobbers.
→ **statistik.arbeitsagentur.de**

Social network to protect against existential risks

Today a tightly woven web of state health, pension, accident, nursing care, and unemployment insurance protects citizens against the consequences of existential risks and threats. Moreover, the social network encompasses a basic income for pensioners and those permanently unable to work as well as fiscal benefits such as the family allowance system (child benefit, tax advantages). Following a further increase in early 2018, families receive 194 euros monthly for the first and second child, 200 euros for the third, and 225 euros for additional children. The Grand Coalition formed in March 2018 intends to increase child benefit again in 2019, namely by 25 euros. The Coalition Agreement also envisages anchoring children's rights in the Basic Law.

The pension package that entered into force in 2014 especially improves the situation of elderly people. The reform saw the introduction, among other things, of the full pension from 63 years of age and the so-called mother's pension, intended to serve

With a monthly child allowance, the state specifically promotes families – pre-school childcare provision has been broadened

as an acknowledgement of mothers' work raising children. Women who raised children born before 1992 did not have the childcare options available to parents today and as such fewer opportunities in the world of work. The mother's pension acknowledges women's work in raising children. Since July 2014 around 9.5 million women (and a small number of men) have received over 300 euros more in pension payments per child per year. Furthermore, since 1 July 2014 people covered by the pension insurance scheme who have paid in for 45 years have been entitled to retire at 63 without their pension being subject to deductions. By the end of February 2018 there had been some 982,000 applications.

Health insurance cover is a legal requirement in Germany. Medical care is guaranteed by a broad spectrum of hospitals, practices, and rehabilitation clinics. ■

PANORAMA

LEISURE TIME AND TRAVEL

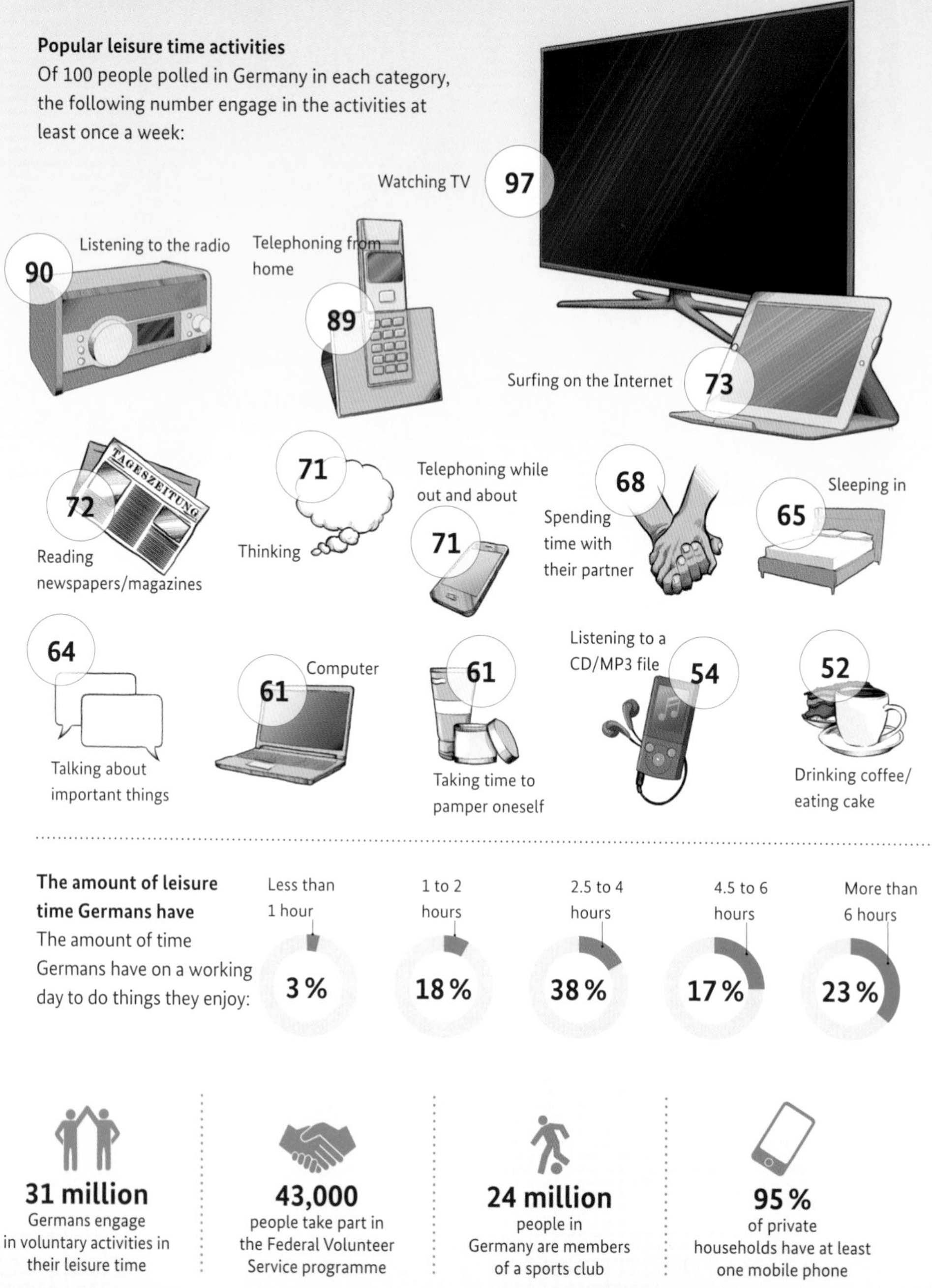

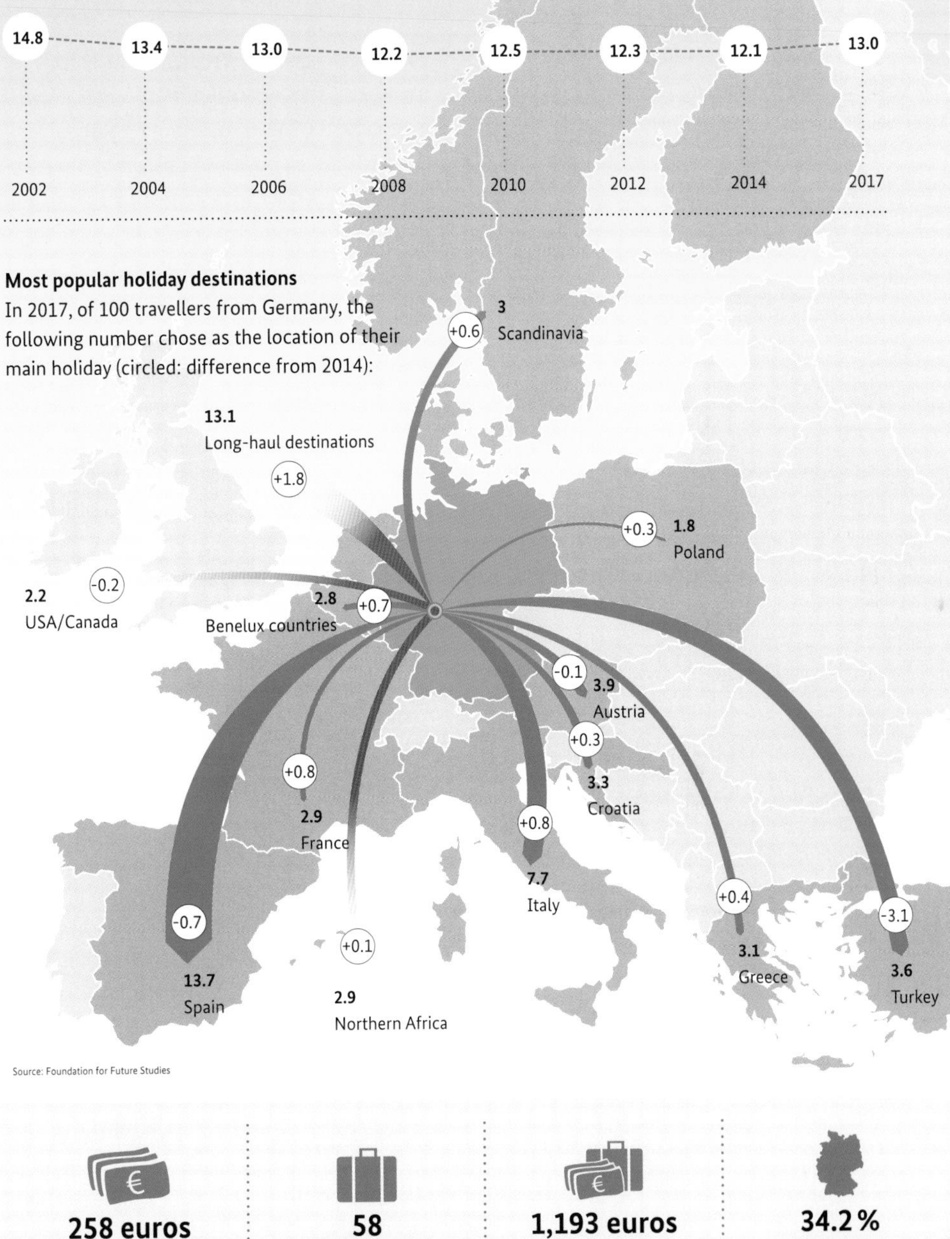

Source: Foundation for Future Studies

258 euros
is what every household spends per month on leisure time, culture, and entertainment

58
of 100 Germans go on a trip each year lasting at least five days

1,193 euros
is the average amount Germans spend on their main vacation

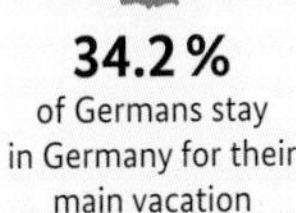

34.2 %
of Germans stay in Germany for their main vacation

TOPIC

FREEDOM OF RELIGIOUS WORSHIP

The religious landscape in Germany is shaped by increasing plurality and secularisation. 55 percent of the German population confesses to one of the two major Christian faiths, organised in the 27 Catholic dioceses and German Bishops' Conference and the Protestant regional churches under the umbrella organisation Evangelical Church in Germany (EKD).

The Catholic Church, with around 24.6 million members in 11,500 parishes, is part of the worldwide Roman Catholic Church headed by the Pope. The EKD is a community of 20 independent evangelical regional churches of the Lutheran, Reformed, and United confessions. With around 23 million members, they encompass the majority of evangelical Christians. About 36 percent of the population does not profess to a particular faith. As a consequence of the ageing membership and high levels of people leaving the Christian churches, the number of believers is falling. In 2016 alone, 162,000 people left the Catholic Church alone. The Evangelical Church reported 190,000 persons leaving. The low number of believers in east Germany is particularly striking.

Islam is gaining in significance for religious life owing to migration. There are an estimated 4-5 million Muslims in Germany from 50 different nations, but there is no central survey. Significant Muslim communities have formed in many cities. The German Islam Conference (DIK) established in 2006 provides an official framework for interaction between Muslims and the German state.

Jewish life in Germany, which was entirely destroyed after the Holocaust, has been revived since the end of the Cold War thanks to migrants from the former USSR. Today around 200,000 Jews live in Germany. Just under 100,000 of them are organised in 105 Jewish communities, which have a broad religious spectrum and are represented by the Central Council of Jews in Germany, founded in 1950.

LIST

- Catholic diocese with the most members: **Archdiocese of Cologne with roughly two million Catholics**
- Evangelical regional church with the most members: **Hanover with more than 2.6 million Protestants**
- Major mosques: **Yavuz Sultan Selim Mosque/Mannheim; Şehitlik Mosque/Berlin, Fatih Mosque/Bremen**
- Largest Jewish community: **Jewish Community of Berlin (10,000)**

In Germany the Basic Law guarantees religious freedom; there are more than 2,000 mosques

Germany has no state church. The basis of the relationship between state and religion is the freedom of religion enshrined in the Basic Law, the separation of church and state in the sense of the state's religious neutrality and the right to self-determination of the religious communities. The state and religious communities cooperate on a joint basis. The state helps finance nurseries and schools sponsored by religious communities, while churches levy a church tax, collected by the state, to finance social services. Schools must offer religious studies as a regular subject (limited in Berlin and Bremen). Islamic religious instruction is currently being expanded. Additional teachers are being trained in order to offer Muslim children and young people who go to school in Germany religious instruction. ■

CULTURE & THE MEDIA

Vibrant Nation of Culture • Innovative Creative Industry • Intercultural Dialogue • Cosmopolitan Positions • Rapid Change in the Media • Exciting World Heritage Sites • Attractive Language

INSIGHT

VIBRANT NATION OF CULTURE

There is no one single German culture. There are many German cultures which simultaneously coexist despite what are often astonishing differences; they are intertwined, repelling and attracting one another. To speak of Germany as a nation of culture in the 21st century is to talk of a mature and continuously developing living organism whose variety is astounding, unsettling, indeed often taxing. This can in part be attributed to the country's federal traditions: After all, Germany was not a unified state until 1871. Not only the Federal Republic of Germany founded in 1949, but also the Germany that was reunified in 1990 has consciously upheld the federal traditions and left the federal states firmly responsible for cultural policy. It was not until 1998 that there was a minister of state in charge of culture and the media attached to the Federal Chancellery. One of the effects of Germany having arisen from many small and medium-sized states and free cities, there are, amongst other things, around 300 theatres and 130 professional orchestras (which are in some instances paired with radio stations). Furthermore, 540 art museums with outstanding international collections form an unprecedented gallery scene. Germany is a world leader in terms of sheer variety in cultural facilities. The population generally welcomes the fact that theatres, orchestras, and museums are predominantly public institutions run by the federal states. Against the backdrop of public budget constraints, sociodemographic change, and shifts in the media landscape (such as digitisation) the cultural system is currently in a phase of upheaval and reorientation.

Germany's reputation as a major cultural nation rests on the great names of the past, ▸

VIDEO AR APP

Culture & The Media: the video on the topic → **tued.net/en/vid7**

The future centre for dialogue between the world's cultures: the Humboldt Forum is under construction in Berlin

such as Bach, Beethoven, and Brahms in music, Goethe, Schiller, and Thomas Mann in literature. Moreover, there are exceptional examples of German Modernists in all art genres.

It bears noting that the country has gone through a process which began earlier in other European nations. Germany has embraced outside influences on the basis of its own traditions and developed a new narrative. Young artists from migratory backgrounds have found expressive means, both poetic and musical, to respond to the encounter and fusion of different cultural backgrounds.

The regional artistic and cultural centres have morphed into vibrant centres of new German culture in the increasingly blurred grey area between low-brow and high-brow culture. Together they create a force field, a reflection of Germany in concentrated form. There is also the Humboldt Forum project, which will open in 2019 as a cultural lighthouse in the rebuilt palace in central Berlin. Characterised by cosmopolitanism, it should facilitate an international exchange of knowledge and intercultural dialogue. ■

INTERNET

Kulturportal Deutschland
Website on selected events and cultural policy issues
→ **kulturserver.de**

Litrix
Multilingual information portal to present German literature worldwide
→ **litrix.de**

Filmportal
Platform on movies in German
→ **filmportal.de**

There are many venues in Germany for the performing arts

COMPACT

PLAYERS & ORGANISATIONS

German Federal Government Commissioner for Culture and the Media

The German Federal Government Commissioner for Culture and the Media, Monika Grütters, is, as Minister of State, a member of the Federal Chancellery. Her tasks include promoting cultural institutions and projects that are of national significance.

→ bundesregierung.de

Goethe-Institut

Goethe-Institut e.V. is Germany's globally active cultural institute. Its brief is to promote a knowledge of the German language abroad, nurture international cultural cooperation, and paint a comprehensive picture of Germany today.

→ goethe.de

Institute for Foreign Cultural Relations

The Institute for Foreign Cultural Relations (ifa) dedicates itself world-wide to interaction on art, civil society dialogue, and providing information on foreign cultural policy.

→ ifa.de

Kulturstiftung des Bundes

The Kulturstiftung des Bundes promotes art and culture that falls within the ambit of the Federal Government. One focal point is supporting innovative programmes and projects in the international context.

→ kulturstiftung-des-bundes.de

Haus der Kulturen der Welt

Haus der Kulturen der Welt in Berlin is a centre of international cultural exchange and a forum for contemporary debates.

→ hkw.de

Deutscher Kulturrat

Deutscher Kulturrat e.V. is the acknowledged umbrella association of German cultural associations, with 258 federal cultural associations and organisations as its members.

→ kulturrat.de

Central Agency for German Schools Abroad

The Central Agency for German Schools Abroad (ZfA) promotes and advises 1,200 schools abroad, including 140 German schools abroad.

→ auslandsschulwesen.de

DIGITAL PLUS

For details on all the topics in this chapter – commented lists of links, articles, documents, speeches; and for further information on keywords such as the Federal Government's responsibility for culture, Kulturstiftung des Bundes, Deutscher Filmpreis, documenta.

→ tued.net/en/dig7

TOPIC

INNOVATIVE CREATIVE INDUSTRY

Culture and the creative industry are among the economy's most innovative sectors. In Germany, their contribution to total economic output (gross value added) is steadily increasing and today is already on a par with major sectors of industry, such as mechanical engineering. Sales by the creative industries, which now embrace some 253,000 companies and in which 1.6 million people work, totalled around 154 billion euros in 2016. The Federal Government intends specifically to strengthen the cultural and creative industries, further developing support schemes and financing options to this end.

The common core of work in culture and the creative industries is the creative act underlying artistic, literary, cultural, musical, architectural, and creative content, works, products, productions, and services. Structurally speaking, the sector is defined by self-employed freelancers, and small or micro-enterprises. They are primarily private-sector based – meaning not first and foremost in the public sector (museums, theatre, orchestras) or part of civil society (arts, associations, foundations). Through the consistent promotion of start-ups, in many cities a raft of service providers has arisen in the fields of design, software, and games in particular. Specifically, the software and games industry relies on interfacing different segments, such as film, video, music, text, and animation, to tap the sector's potential and in 2016 this spawned total sales of 29 billion euros. The Berlin-Brandenburg region leads the way, with a good 200 companies. No other area has such a concentrated gaming infrastructure, including the relevant colleges. That said, Frankfurt am Main, Hamburg, Leipzig, Cologne, and Munich all have distinct creative industry clusters. ■

DIAGRAM

Sector with great potential
The cultural and creative industries bring traditional segments of business together with new technologies and modern forms of ICT. In Germany they include 12 subsegments: the music business, bookselling, the art market, the film industry, radio, the fine arts, architecture, design, the press, advertising, software/games, others.

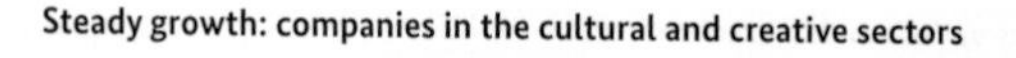

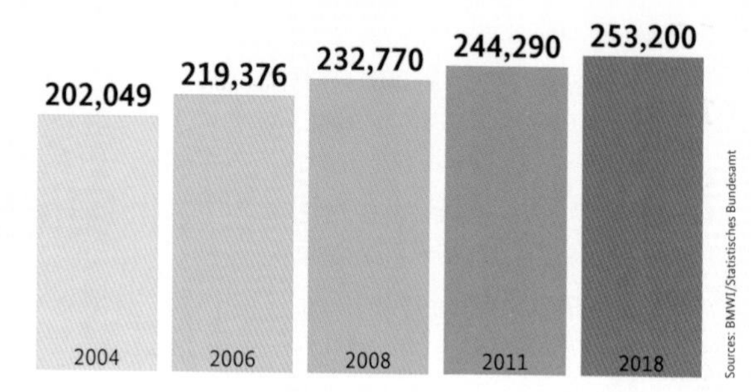

Berlin is considered the start-up capital, among young entrepreneurs, too

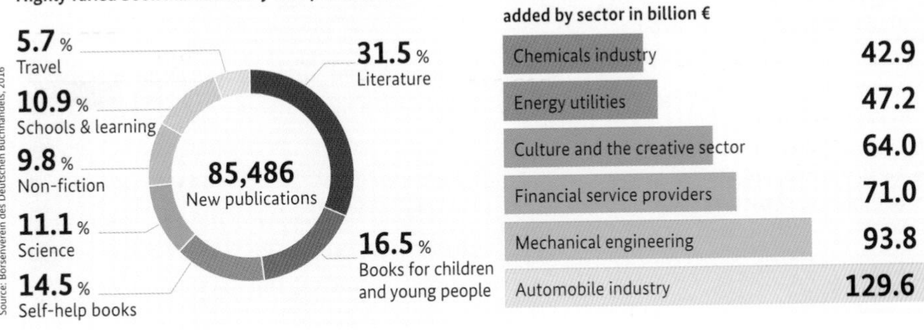

TOPIC

INTERCULTURAL DIALOGUE

Alongside classical diplomacy and foreign economic policy, cultural relations and education policy form the third pillar of German foreign policy. Its key objectives include laying strong foundations for relations to other countries and fostering dialogue among people and peoples by means of exchanges and cooperation in the fields of culture, education, and scholarship. The foreign cultural policy thus paves the way for mutual understanding, an important bedrock for policies committed to the peaceful settlement of differences. Other tasks include promoting the German language around the world, showcasing Germany as a country with a successful and diverse cultural scene, and communicating a contemporary image of Germany abroad.

LIST

- Largest art museum: **Hamburger Kunsthalle**
- Largest orchestra: **Gewandhausorchester Leipzig**
- Largest movie theatre: **Cinemaxx in Essen**
- Largest theatre stage: **Friedrichstadtpalast (Berlin)**
- Largest festival hall: **Baden-Baden**

Current initiatives include promoting a variety of cultural programmes, such as exhibitions, guest performances by German theatres, supporting literature and films, and projects in dialogue with the Islamic world as well as kulturweit, a scheme that enables young people from Germany to spend a year doing voluntary service abroad.

The programmes and projects rest on a comprehensive understanding of culture

The Federal Foreign Office only implements the smallest part of its cultural relations policy itself. It primarily entrusts these tasks to intermediary organisations active as entities under private law and each with its own special focus. They include the Goethe-Institut, Institute for Foreign Cultural Relations (ifa), the German Academic Exchange Service (DAAD), the German Commission for UNESCO, and the Alexander von Humboldt Foundation (on foreign education policy, please turn to the chapter on Education and Knowledge).

The work of the cultural intermediaries is defined in agreements on goals, but they are largely free to structure the programmes and projects themselves. The Goethe-Institut has a total of 159 institutes in 98 different countries. It promotes a knowledge of the German language abroad and nurtures international cultural cooperation. The ifa dedicates itself

Old manuscripts from Timbuktu (Mali) are being preserved and researched thanks to Federal Foreign Office funding

mainly to cultural dialogue – in the form of exhibitions and conferences. The current trends in cultural dialogue: digital cultural and intermediary services and the new opportunities for interactive participation. In all the projects, since the 1970s foreign cultural policy has emphasised a holistic, non-elitist concept of culture that does not limit "culture" to "art".

That said, the focus is not just on German culture. The preservation of cultural heritage programmes supports upholding important historical cultural assets worldwide. For example, from 1981 to 2016 the Federal Foreign Office helped fund some 2,800 projects in 144 countries, including the preservation of the Timbuktu manuscripts in Mali, the creation of a digital registry of cultural assets for Syria, the digitisation of traditional music in Cameroon, and the restoration of Borobudur Temple in Indonesia. ■

TOPIC

COSMOPOLITAN POSITIONS

In German society, which is steeped in pluralism, there can just as little be one predominant cultural trend as there can be one metropolis that towers over all the others. Buttressed by the country's federal structure, Germany is typified by the simultaneity of many exceptionally different things from different periods, indeed even countervailing or competing currents – in theatre, film, music, the visual arts, and literature.

There is a clear trend in theatre: The number of premiere performances by contemporary playwrights has soared. They run the entire gamut of current forms of the performing arts, in which traditional spoken theatre mingles with pantomime, dance, video, play acting, and music, giving rise to dense performance-like, post-drama stage work. The sheer variety presented each year at the May Berlin Theatertreffen can be read as the polyphonic response to the issues raised by a complex reality.

Alongside the cultural mainstream driven by the centre-ground in society new things are arising, increasingly from marginalised sections of society, and these ideas are penetrating and enriching the established world of theatre. "Postmigrant" is the buzzword describing the phenomenon, reflecting that Germany is an immigration society as is visible in many cities, especially in Berlin. Millions of Germans with a migrant background are the second or third generation of their family living here; they tell tales of themselves and the lives of their parents and grandparents, unlike the stories told by citizens who have lived in Germany for centuries. Whether they were born in Germany or not, as a rule they are not influenced by some hands-on experience of immigration, but by the experience of cultural hybridity. This life in various cultural contexts engenders new forms of artistic enquiry into society and draws up new front lines for negotiating rights, a sense of belonging, or participation. New narratives arise that encourage society to view itself in a new light and define how German culture is perceived abroad.

A beacon of such art that celebrates trans-culturalism is Shermin Langhoff's Post-Migrant

INFO

German Digital Library

The German Digital Library (DDB) is, closely networked with the European virtual library Europeana.eu, a portal cataloguing Germany's cultural heritage. This encompasses cultural treasures such as manuscripts, historical films, music, and digitised books. The library already contains more than 18 million items. The long-term goal is for up to 30,000 cultural and academic institutions from all spheres and disciplines to be networked within the DDB.

→ **deutsche-digitale-bibliothek.de**

Yael Ronen's production of Common Ground at the Maxim Gorki Theatre made a real splash

Theatre in Berlin's Maxim Gorki Theatre, the city's smallest state theatre, but one with a long-standing tradition. Langhoff's shows reach out well beyond traditional theatre-goers and have successfully attracted a new and primarily young clientele; they reflect an opaque process that is constantly shifting and becoming more differentiated. In 2015 and 2016, the Gorki Theatre was invited to present the plays "Common Ground", which addresses the war in the Balkans, and "The Situation" about the Middle-Eastern conflict, both produced by Israeli director Yael Ronen, at the Berlin Theatertreffen. Theatre is thus now doing what has long since taken place in the worlds of Pop music and literature. Here, too, the biographies of the artists reflect society's diversity, presenting exciting fusions of widely differing styles to offer new perspectives. In Pop, a whole array of international ▸

styles of music, ranging from Balkan beats, African-American sounds, and Turkish Saz Rock to American Hip Hop and even Techno, blends with other strands or electronic elements that are considered "typically German". As in other countries, Rap is a point of identification for young people from migrant families, with languages often blurring in the process.

The son of Turkish immigrants, director Fatih Akin has made it right to the top. In 2018 he won a Golden Globe for his drama "In the Fade", starring German Hollywood actress Diane Kruger. In his films, Akin does not shy away from sensitive issues of living together and in conflict, and has milieus and clichés collide. Post-migrant Germany is not necessarily cosy, but it is exciting and dynamic.

Post-migrant themes play a key role in contemporary literature

For many years, as a matter of course there have been important authors with migrant backgrounds among the most successful authors writing in German. They include Navid Kermani, who in 2015 won one of Germany's most illustrious cultural prizes, the Peace Prize of the German Book Trade, and is known for both his fiction and his books on religious tolerance, as well as Katja Petrowskaya, Sherko Fatah, Nino Haratischwili, Saša Stanišić, Feridun Zaimoglu, and Alina Bronsky, to name but a few. Their books, which reflect among other things on their experiences with their Iranian, Russian, and Turkish backgrounds, are eagerly read and their works transport the specific themes and experiences of migration into the heart of society, where they are regularly discussed.

Fatih Akin's drama "In the Fade" starring Diane Kruger won a Golden Globe in 2018

MAP

Important cultural awards in Germany

❶ Golden Bear
The Berlin International Film Festival: one of the world's key film festivals next to Venice and Cannes. A Golden Bear and several Silver Bears are awarded.

❷ Preis der Leipziger Buchmesse
Preis der Leipziger Buchmesse is a book prize awarded to a new publication in German.

❸ Deutscher Filmpreis
Featuring prize money totalling almost 3 million euros, Deutscher Filmpreis is the best-endowed German cultural prize.

❹ German Book Prize
A jury chooses the best novel written in German that year.

❺ Georg Büchner Preis
The Georg Büchner Preis is the pre-eminent literature prize for Germany, Austria, and Switzerland.

The visual arts in Germany are likewise cosmopolitan and international. As the statistics of the new intake at German art academies and colleges shows: Since 2013, the annual number of foreign students enrolling for the first semester has exceeded that of Germans. Today Berlin, with about 500 galleries and its many spaces for presenting artistic positions, is considered the metropolis for young, contemporary art that features strongly in the Berlin Art Week, when all over the city venues present the latest artistic ideas. Indeed, Germany's capital is today undoubtedly one of the world's largest hubs where contemporary art is produced. This is demonstrated every two years at the Venice Biennale, and not just in the German Pavilion there: A large number of the international artists exhibited in the city on the lagoon state that they live in Berlin. ■

TOPIC

RAPID CHANGE IN THE MEDIA

Freedom of the press and the media is guaranteed at a very high level in Germany, and is protected by the constitution. Article 5 of the Basic Law states: "Every person shall have the right freely to express and disseminate his opinions in speech, writing, and pictures, and to inform himself without hindrance from generally accessible sources. ... There shall be no censorship." The Press Freedom Index compiled by the NGO Reporter ohne Grenzen ranks Germany 16th of 180 countries in 2017. There is a diversity of opinions and a pluralism of information. The press is not controlled by governments or parties, as private-sector media corporations are responsible for it. The public broadcasters based on the British model (ARD, ZDF, Deutschlandfunk) as corporate bodies paid for from licensing fees and as public-sector entities are the second pillar of the media world, which rests on the dual principle of private and public-sector entities that has essentially remained unchanged since the foundation of the Federal Republic of Germany in 1949. As of 2015, the monthly license fee has been 17.50 euros. Since the 1980s, there has been a whole raft of private radio and TV broadcasters in the market. The most important TV news programmes are Tagesschau and Tagesthemen, both on ARD, heute and heute journal on ZDF, and RTL aktuell. In Berlin alone, which is among the 10 top media cities worldwide, there are 900 accredited parliamentary correspondents and 440 foreign correspondents from 60 different countries on the ground.

The many different media voices include around 300 daily newspapers, mainly distributed regionally, 20 weeklies, and 1,600 mass-market magazines. After China, India, Japan, and the USA, Germany is the fifth-largest newspaper market worldwide. Per publication ▸

MILESTONES

1945
After the end of Nazi rule, in Germany initially newspapers may only appear under Allied licence. In the US zone of occupation the first licence is awarded on 1 August 1945 to the Frankfurter Rundschau.

1950
The six West German broadcasting houses agree in Bremen to join forces to form the "Arbeitsgemeinschaft der öffentlich-rechtlichen Rundfunkanstalten der Bundesrepublik Deutschland," or ARD broadcaster.

1984
In Ludwigshafen the Programmgesellschaft für Kabel- und Satellitenrundfunk, or PKS for short, starts broadcasting. This marks the birth of private TV channels in Germany.

Social media are fundamentally changing the structure of the media, communications patterns, and the public sphere

1995

The first German newspaper, namely the leftist/liberal taz, goes online only six years after the foundation of the World Wide Web. After its go-live, the membership of the digitaz community surges.

1997

About 4.1 million German citizens over the age of 14 use the new online access channels at least occasionally. In 2014, the figure rises to around 55.6 million, or 79.1 percent of the over-14s in Germany.

2018

Some 21 million people in Germany use Facebook on a weekly basis. 1.8 million regularly use Twitter, 5.6 million Instagram. The leading social media site is WhatsApp, with 40 million weekly users.

Germany's largest newsroom: the central editorial desk at Deutsche Presse-Agentur (dpa) in Berlin

▸ day, 16.1 million dailies and five million weekly or Sunday papers are sold (2016). The leading nationwide newspapers are Süddeutsche Zeitung, Frankfurter Allgemeine Zeitung, Die Welt, Die Zeit, taz, and Handelsblatt, and all stand out for investigative research, analysis, background, and comprehensive commentary. News magazine Spiegel/Spiegel Online and the yellow-press publication Bild are considered the most-quoted media.

At the same time, the sector is undergoing a profound structural change. For the last 15 years, newspapers have been regularly losing on average 1.5-2 percent of their paid printed editions. They are increasingly rarely reaching younger readers and with circulation

DIAGRAM

Everyday digital life
Mobile Internet access and the use of mobile handhelds are surging in Germany. With the increase in mobile accessing of data, technological requirements likewise grow as regards network infrastructure. Studies also show that the number of Internet users has for some time now only been edging up.

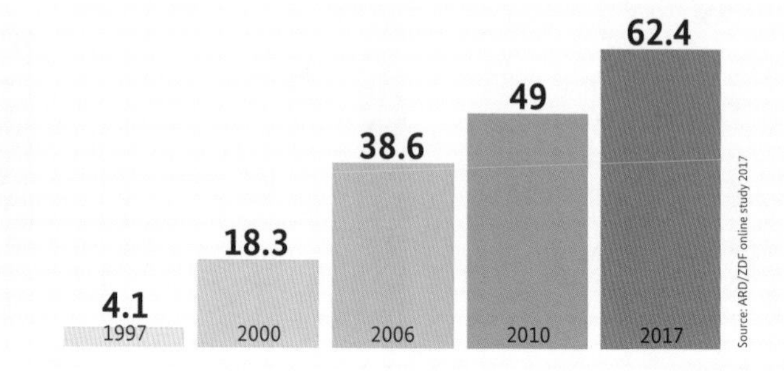

figures and advertising revenues dwindling are in difficult waters. Over 100 newspapers have responded to the free-for-view Internet by introducing pay-on-demand systems. The publishing industry is in flux – amongst other things because meanwhile almost 800,000 newspaper copies sold daily are distributed digitally and the number of digital subscriptions is continually rising.

Digitisation of the media world, the Internet, the rampant growth in mobile handhelds, and the triumphs of social media have significantly changed how the media are used. Today, 62.4 million Germans over the age of 14 (89.8 percent) are online. More than 50 million people use the Internet daily. On average, every user spends about 165 minutes a day online; more than every second person surfs from a mobile handheld. Moreover, over half of all Internet users are members of a private community. The digital revolution has generated a new concept of the public sphere; social media and the Bloggosphere mirror an open society of dialogue in which everyone can participate in opinion-forming discourse. Whether the interactive Internet nodes where people gather also form the foundations for a viable future digital journalism remains to be seen. Journalists from all fields are living up to their professional responsibility to counter fake news and deliberate disinformation. ■

GLOBAL

Deutsche Welle Deutsche Welle (DW) is Germany's foreign radio service and a member of ARD, the public radio and TV broadcasting association. DW broadcasts in 30 different languages, provides TV programming (DW-TV), radio, Internet services, and supporting media development through the DW Akademie. The German News Service provides free news in four languages for interested individuals and media.
→ dw.com

DW

Multiple access: how Germans use the Internet

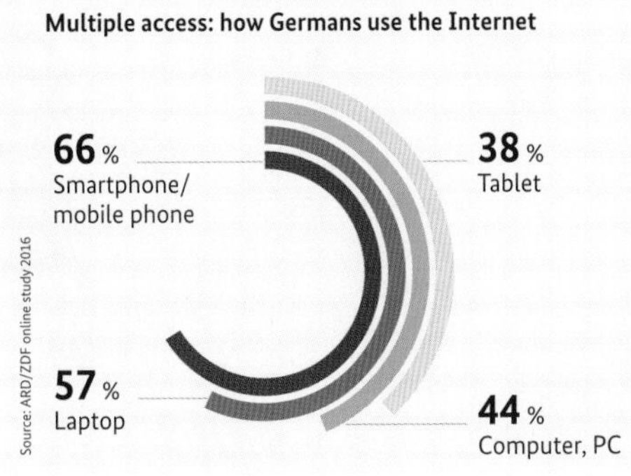

Daily media usage

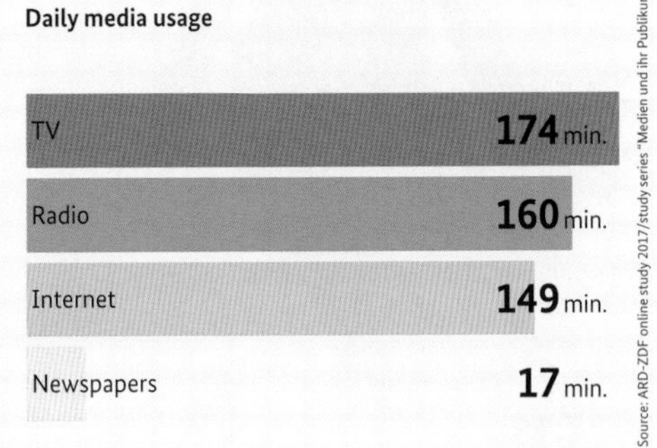

PANORAMA

EXCITING WORLD HERITAGE SITES

17 Cologne Cathedral
This masterpiece of Gothic architecture was built down through many generations – from 1248 to 1880.

21 Wartburg
Reformer Martin Luther translated the New Testament into German inside the protection of its walls.

25 Zollverein Coal Mine Industrial Complex
This complex in Essen where operations were discontinued in 1986 stands for the development of heavy industry in Europe.

18 Bauhaus
The Bauhaus sites in Dessau and Weimar stand for the famous early 20th-century design college.

157 m
Height of Cologne Cathedral

1 km²
Area of the Zollverein Coal Mine Industrial Complex

44 km²
Area covered by ancient beech forests

2,300,000
Visitors to Museum Island

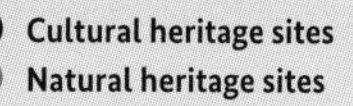

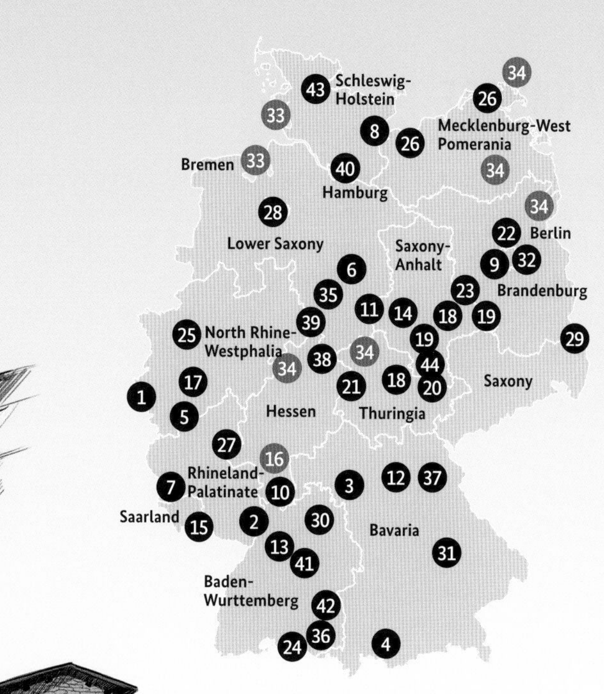

1 Aachen Cathedral
2 Speyer Cathedral
3 Würzburg Residence with the Court Gardens and Residence Square
4 Pilgrimage Church of Wies
5 Castles of Augustusburg and Falkenlust at Brühl
6 St Mary's Cathedral and St Michael's Church at Hildesheim
7 Roman Monuments, Cathedral of St Peter and Church of Our Lady in Trier
8 Hanseatic City of Lübeck
9 Palaces and Parks of Potsdam and Berlin
10 Abbey and Altenmünster of Lorsch
11 Mines of Rammelsberg, Historic Town of Goslar and Upper Harz Water Management System
12 Town of Bamberg
13 Maulbronn Monastery Complex
14 Collegiate Church, Castle and Old Town of Quedlinburg
15 Völklingen Ironworks
16 Messel Pit Fossil Site
17 Cologne Cathedral
18 Bauhaus and its sites in Weimar and Dessau
19 Luther Memorials in Eisleben and Wittenberg
20 Classical Weimar
21 Wartburg Castle
22 Museumsinsel (Museum Island), Berlin
23 Garden Kingdom of Dessau-Wörlitz
24 Monastic Island of Reichenau
25 Zollverein Coal Mine Industrial Complex in Essen
26 Historic Centres of Stralsund and Wismar
27 Upper Middle Rhine Valley
28 Town Hall and Roland on the Marketplace of Bremen
29 Muskauer Park / Park Mużakowski
30 Frontiers of the Roman Empire
31 Old town of Regensburg with Stadtamhof
32 Berlin Modernism Housing Estates
33 Wadden Sea
34 Ancient Beech Forests of Germany
35 Fagus Factory in Alfeld
36 Prehistoric pile dwellings around the Alps
37 Margravial Opera House Bayreuth
38 Bergpark Wilhelmshöhe
39 Carolingian Westwork and Civitas Corvey
40 Speicherstadt and Kontorhaus District with Chilehaus
41 Le Corbusier's architecture (Weissenhofsiedlung in Stuttgart)
42 Caves and Ice Age art in the Swabian Alb region
43 Archaeological Border complex of Hedeby and the Danevirke
44 Naumburg Cathedral

30 Frontiers of the Roman Empire
The Saalburg castle within the Roman frontier wall in Hessen has been reconstructed.

34 Ancient Beech Forests
Five beech forests in Germany are included on the UNESCO World Heritage List.

2,000
Half-timbered buildings in Quedlinburg

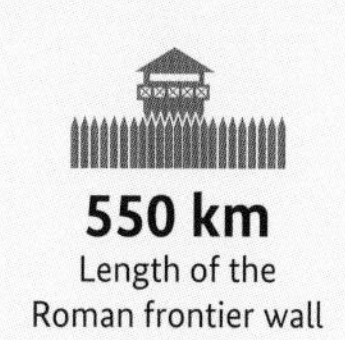

550 km
Length of the Roman frontier wall

10,000
Different animal and plant species in the Wadden Sea

1,073
UNESCO World Heritage sites worldwide

TOPIC

ATTRACTIVE LANGUAGE

German is one of the 15 or so Germanic languages, a branch of the Indo-European language family. About 130 million people in Germany, Austria, Switzerland, Luxembourg, Belgium, Liechtenstein, and South Tyrol (Italy) speak German natively or as a regularly used second language. It is therefore the most widely spoken native language in the EU and one of the ten most widely spoken languages. The 2015 survey on 'German as a foreign language worldwide' refers to a total of 15.4 million people currently learning German as a second language. The number of people globally who actually speak German as a foreign language can be roughly estimated at about 100 million.

One reason why German's importance is disproportionally high relative to the number of people speaking it stems from the country's economic strength, which makes the language very desirable. This desirability is helping drive an active policy of spreading the German language: by supporting language teaching facilities in Germany and abroad, providing scholarships or making academic offers to mobile international students. It is also clear from the significantly increasing interest in German, especially in the rising powers of China, India, and Brazil as well as in other fast-growing areas of the Asian continent, where in places demand has quadrupled since 2010.

#NUMBER

16

major dialect associations exist in Germany, including, for example, Bavarian, Alemannic, Westphalian, Brandenburg, and Northern Low German. The regional differences in spoken language are fairly large; in general the importance of dialects is dwindling.

Important institutions for learning German include the 140 German schools outside Germany and the almost 2,000 schools that lay emphasis on German lessons, which are included in the Federal Foreign Office's initiative, Schools: Partners for the Future (PASCH). In 2016, around 278,000 people took language courses at the Goethe-Institut, which offers German as a foreign language and language tests in more than 90 countries. With free e-learning programmes, videos, audio and print material, Deutsche Welle offers online German courses for beginners and advanced speakers.

By contrast, the relevance of German as a language of international scholarship is essentially declining. The global share of articles in German in scientific publications is

The German language is the most-frequently spoken mother tongue in the European Union

only one percent in bibliographic databases. German enjoys greater importance as an academic language in the humanities and social sciences. Non-German-speaking scholars very rarely publish in German, whereas German-speaking scholars publish extensively in English. Yet on the Internet, German plays an important role. With regard to the most-used languages based on websites, German ranked third, far behind English, but only just behind Russian.

Globalisation is exerting pressure on all international languages, and this is serving to appreciably further strengthen the position of English as the world language. Nonetheless, German will remain an important international language. ■

WAY OF LIFE

Land of Diversity • Urban Quality of Life • Sustainable Tourism • Sporting Challenges • Attractions in Berlin • Leisurely Enjoyment

INSIGHT

LAND OF DIVERSITY

A love of nature and cities alike, healthy food and gourmet restaurants, a strong sense of tradition and a cosmopolitan mind-set – measuring 357,000 square kilometres, Germany is the fourth largest country in the European Union (EU) after France, Spain, and Sweden. From the North and Baltic Seas to the Alps in the south, Germany is geographically sub-divided into the North German Lowlands, the Mittelgebirge ridge, the Central Uplands in southwest Germany, the South German Alpine foothills, and the Bavarian Alps. From north to south the greatest distance is 876 kilometres, from east to west 640 kilometres.

Germany is one of the countries with the highest standards of living in the world. The 2016 United Nations' Human Development Index (HDI) puts Germany fourth out of a total of 188 countries. With 82.6 million inhabitants, Germany is the most populous country in the EU and one of the most densely populated; around 77 percent of its inhabitants live in densely and highly populated areas. Around 30 percent of the population resides in big cities with more than 100,000 inhabitants, of which there are 80 in Germany; Munich has 4,713 people per square kilometre, Berlin 4,012. Experts believe the ongoing trend of growth and innovation is reflected in the renaissance of cities, and forecast that by 2030 the number of inhabitants in major cities will have surged – with considerable consequences for the housing market, inner-city mobility, and infrastructure. In particular, the 18-to-24-year-old age bracket is showing a pronounced willingness to move to cities. This urbanisation makes Germany part of a global trend. The cities are also great tourist attractions – Berlin especially is developing ▸

VIDEO AR APP

Way of life: the video on the topic

→ **tued.net/en/vid8**

Sylt, the fourth-largest German island, offers kilometres of sandy beaches along the North Sea coast

▸ into a real magnet and is currently setting one visitor record after another. In the European rankings for the absolute number of overnight stays, Berlin, with its 3.7 million inhabitants, places third behind London and Paris.

At the same time, however, this longing for urban life contrasts with a strong call for things regional – in particular when it comes to what Germans eat. The organic food industry is firmly established in German agriculture, generating sales of organic products worth around 10 billion euros annually. Indeed, 29,174 organic farms, almost 10 percent of agricultural enterprises, cultivate 7.1 percent of agricultural land. The organic products are supported by certifications (around 75,000 products boast the German state organic seal), extensive consumer protection laws, and comprehensive marking obligations. In 2016, some 8 million people in Germany referred to themselves as vegetarians; 1.3 million said they live a vegan lifestyle. Gourmets, however, do not miss out. This is thanks to the 300 restaurants in Germany with one or more stars in the 2018 Guide Michelin – more than ever before. ■

→ INTERNET

Destatis
Data, facts, and official statistical studies, compiled by the German Federal Statistical Office in Wiesbaden
→ **destatis.de**

OECD
Comparison of the material living conditions and the quality of life in 38 countries based on the Better Life Index of the Organisation for Economic Co-operation and Development (OECD)
→ **oecdbetterlifeindex.org**

Frankfurt am Main, home to the European Central Bank (ECB), is the only major German city to boast a skyline

COMPACT

PLAYERS & ORGANISATIONS

German National Tourist Board

For over 60 years the German National Tourist Board (DZT) has been working internationally on behalf of the Federal Government to promote Germany as a travel destination. In 2018, the DZT is focussing on hospitality and food culture in the theme year “Culinary Germany”. In 2019 the focal theme will be “100 Years of the Bauhaus”.

→ germany.travel

German Olympic Sports Confederation

The German Olympic Sports Confederation (DOSB) is the umbrella organisation of German sport. It has more than 27 million members in around 91,000 sports clubs.

→ dosb.de

German Football Association

With over 7 million members, the German Football Association (DFB) is the world’s largest national sports federation – and the only football association where both the men’s and the women’s team have won the World Cup.

→ dfb.de

International Sports Promotion

International Sports Promotion has been part of the Federal Republic of Germany’s cultural relations and education activities abroad since 1961. Since then it has supported 1,400 projects in over 100 countries. It primarily promotes sports for women, youth, and people with disabilities, in an effort to advance integration.

→ dosb.de/sportentwicklung/internationales

German Wine Institute

The German Wine Institute (DWI) is the German wine industry’s communications and marketing arm. Its main task is to promote the quality and sales of German wine.

→ deutscheweine.de

Gut leben in Deutschland

In 2015, the Federal Government conducted a dialogue with the people of Germany about their view of the quality of life in the country. It resulted in 46 quality-of-life indicators, which are continually updated and enable “living well” to be measured.

→ gut-leben-in-deutschland.de

DIGITAL PLUS

More information about all the topics in the chapter – annotated link lists, articles, documents; plus more detailed information about terms such as German cuisine, wines from Germany, Bauhaus architecture, wellness holidays in Germany.

→ tued.net/en/dig8

TOPIC

URBAN QUALITY OF LIFE

Good jobs, a clean environment, low crime rates, lots of leisure-time and cultural attractions, good transport links: German cities frequently boast precisely these features. In a 2018 study aimed at evaluating the quality of life in 231 large cities conducted by the Mercer consulting firm, seven German cities place in the Top 30. With Munich (3rd place), Düsseldorf (6), and Frankfurt am Main (7), three actually make the Top Ten. Berlin (13), Hamburg (19), Nuremberg (23), and Stuttgart (28) are also well up the list. In Germany there are 80 large cities (more than 100,000 inhabitants) and 614 medium-sized cities with between 20,000 and 99,999 inhabitants; 75.5 percent of people now live in cities.

The demand for urban living space has led to a sharp rise in rents in the case of first-time lets, and in the price of real estate. With regard to European home ownership rates, Germany comes second from last. Forty-five percent of households live in their own four walls. The majority opt for rented accommodation, which has traditionally always been preferred. Almost 14 percent of people view the cost of living as a "heavy financial burden". On average, such costs absorb 27 percent of monthly incomes. For this reason the Federal Government has paved the way for rent caps aimed at preserving social diversity in regions where the housing market is under pressure. In the event of a change in tenant, new rents are capped at a max. 10 percent higher than for a comparable flat – but there are exceptions. In 2018 the Federal Government has set itself the goal of building 1.5 million new flats and houses in the context of a "housing offensive" and allocated two billion euros for social housing construction. Moreover, families now receive a state subsidy when buying their own home. ■

DIAGRAM

How Germans live

More than half of the people in Germany live in rented accommodation, not in their own four walls. 66 percent of all residential buildings are single-family dwellings, only 6 percent are larger structures with seven or more flats. 35 percent of flats and houses are 100 square metres in size or bigger, only 5.5 percent of flats are smaller than 40 square metres.

Consumer spending by private households in Germany

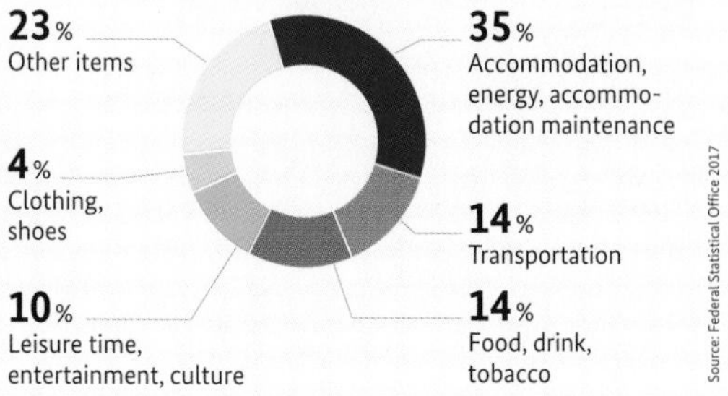

Urban quality of life is in vogue, which is why rents are rising in cities

Share of the population living in cities

Germany	75.5 %
USA	81.8 %
Canada	82.0 %
Great Britain	82.8 %
Australia	89.6 %

Sources: World Bank, Federal and State Stat. Offices 2017

Flats in Germany by number of rooms

Share	Rooms
40.3 %	5 and more rooms
25.4 %	4 rooms
21.7 %	3 rooms
9.2 %	2 rooms
3.3 %	1 room

TOPIC

SUSTAINABLE TOURISM

Germans like to travel. In their own country as well, indeed especially there. After all, for years now the Alps, the coasts, the North German lakes, nature reserves, and river valleys have headed the list of destinations. Germans have long since shared a passion for the diversity of the countryside, and for sightseeing, sport and relaxation options with a continually growing flow of visitors and tourists from abroad. Germany has for years been gaining popularity as a tourist destination.

In 2017, the number of overnights rose to 459 million; guests from abroad accounted for 83.9 million (18.2 percent), which was a record. Tourism experts forecast a rise to 121.5 million by 2030. The positive trend in tourism to Germany began immediately after German Reunification back in 1990 and has since led to a steady rise in the number of overnight stays by foreign guests – by around 88 percent. A good 75 percent of all foreign guests come from Europe, primarily from the Netherlands, Switzerland, Great Britain, and Italy. 7.5 percent come from the USA.

At the same time the number of visitors from Asia and Africa is rising. From 2015 to 2016, their market share rose by some 8 percent in each case. In Europe, since 2010 Germany has been second in the league of most popular destinations among Europeans – after Spain and ahead of France. Seasonal distribution reveals peak figures from June to October during the high season, and regional distribution very high numbers for Bavaria, Berlin, and Baden-Württemberg. Germany is an attractive country to visit for young people aged between 15 and 34, who contribute to the positive trend in tourism.

A successful trade fair and congress centre

In 2017, for the 13th time in a row, Germany maintained its position as the no. 1 conference and congress centre in Europe. In the international congress centre rankings, Germany is in second place behind the USA.

LIST

- Biggest airport: **Frankfurt am Main**
- Biggest railway station: **Leipzig**
- Biggest port: **Hamburg**
- Biggest trade fair grounds: **Hanover**
- Biggest spa resort: **Wiesbaden**
- Biggest public festival: **Oktoberfest**
- Biggest amusement park: **Europa-Park, Rust**

An attractive Alpine panorama: The many foreign tourists who visit Bavaria appreciate the idyll

In 2016, some 113,000 international exhibitors and 3.2 million international guests came to trade fairs in Germany, which is regarded as the most important trade fair location worldwide. In particular the "magic cities" of Berlin, Dresden, Düsseldorf, Frankfurt am Main, Hamburg, Hanover, Leipzig, Cologne, Munich, Nuremberg, and Stuttgart are the magnets for foreign guests. First and foremost among them is Berlin, which in 2016 recorded 12.7 million visitors, and over 31 million overnights. In terms of absolute figures for overnight stays the city is in third place in Europe after London and Paris.

According to a survey conducted by the German National Tourist Board the top international visitor attractions include classics such as Neuschwanstein Castle and ▸

▸ Cologne Cathedral. The numerous UNESCO World Heritage sites, among them Sanssouci Palace in Potsdam and Classical Weimar, are also popular. In addition, events such as the Oktoberfest in Munich, with around 6.2 million visitors the world's biggest public festival, also attract visitors. A football stadium is also on the list of tourist magnets: the Allianz Arena, a masterpiece by Swiss architects Herzog & de Meuron, and the Bayern Munich home ground.

Like culture, movement in general plays a big role in Germany's appeal. Around 200,000 kilometres long, the network of hiking trails alone offers extremely good conditions and magnificent views, for example on routes through the national parks or against the backdrop of the magnificent Alps. On top of this there are more than 200 well-established long-distance cycle trails covering 70,000 kilometres, for example the Iron Curtain Trail (1,131 kilometres) or the 818-kilometre-long German Limes Cycle Route. Those looking for a cheap night's accommodation will find plenty of opportunities, for example in one of the 500 youth hostels, 130 of which are family youth hostels, or on one of the 2,919 campsites.

INFO

Climate In Germany a warm, moderate rainy climate with westerly winds prevails. Major fluctuations in temperature are rare. There is rainfall throughout the year. Mild winters (2 °C to −6 °C) and not too hot summers (18 °C to 20 °C) are the rule. In 2014, the mean annual temperature reached a record 10.3 °C, which was 2.1 degrees above the long-term average of 8.2 °C for the international reference period 1961 to 1990. 2014 was 0.4 degrees warmer than the previous warmest years 2000 and 2007.
→ dwd.de

Feel-good holidays and environmentally friendly travel

Wellness is an important topic in Germany. It includes such unusual features as the river sauna in the Emser Therme thermal complex, as well as the numerous feel-good facilities in spa resorts such as Bad Wörishofen and Bad Oeynhausen, with its Wilhelminian-era architecture. In Germany, there are over 350 spa resorts, which use a label recognised by the "Deutscher Heilbäderverband", the German Association of Spa Resorts. The quality of the medical treatment and support also attracts numerous guests to Germany.

Ever more frequently, travellers are not only taking care of their own wellbeing, but are also paying attention to the environment. In Germany, the demand for ecological tourism and sustainable travel is growing. Organic farms offer holiday rooms, there are 104 nature parks and 17 biosphere reserves, in which great importance is attached to sustainable development and biodiversity. In order for everyone to be able to move around easily in Germany countless initiatives ensure that the disabled too can travel without hindrance.

MAP

Travelling within Germany

• The top destinations
The 11 “magic cities” have a market share of around 43 percent of all overnight stays by foreign guests in Germany. Berlin lies clearly ahead of Munich, Frankfurt am Main, and Hamburg. 56 percent of overnights by foreigners are in cities with 100,000 inhabitants.

✈ The most important airports
The three biggest airports in Germany are in Frankfurt am Main with 64.5 million passengers, Munich with 44.6 million, and Düsseldorf with 24.5 million in 2017.

★ The most popular attractions
According to a survey by the German National Tourist Board, in 2017 the three most popular attractions among foreign tourists were Miniatur Wunderland in Hamburg, the Europa-Park theme park in Rust, and Neuschwanstein Castle.

Attractive tourist destinations in the former East Germany

The five federal states that formerly made up East Germany play a major role in tourism. After Reunification, tourism proved to be an opportunity for many regions in eastern Germany to put themselves on a sound economic footing. Areas of countryside such as the Spreewald biosphere reserve, cultural centres with long-standing traditions such as Dresden and Weimar, and Baltic seaside resorts such as Binz on the island of Rügen attract tourists from Germany and abroad.

Since 1993, the number of overnight stays in eastern Germany has more than doubled. With a market share of 5.1 percent, in 2017 Mecklenburg-Western Pomerania in the north east just pipped the state of Bavaria in the south (with 4.9 percent) in terms of holiday trips of more than five days’ duration. No matter how much one has already seen – as a travel destination Germany still has more to discover, experience, celebrate, and marvel at. ■

TOPIC

SPORTING CHALLENGES

Germany is a country of sports enthusiasts and indeed a successful sporting nation. In the Olympic Games all-time medals table Germany, with 1,757 medals (as at 2018), places third behind the USA and the Russian Federation. Around 28 million people in Germany are members of one of the roughly 91,000 sports clubs. Alongside their sporting duties, the clubs also assume important social and inclusive roles. Particularly as regards youth work and integration they reinforce values such as fair play, team spirit, and tolerance. Given the rising internationalisation of the population, the work done by sports clubs is becoming ever more important with a view to the social integration of migrants. Around 60,700 clubs have members with a migratory background in their teams. Overall it is safe to assume that approximately 1.7 million people with a migratory background are members of a sports club. Nonetheless, the group of people with a migratory background is still under-represented in organised sport.

The German Olympic Sports Confederation's "Integration through Sport" programme believes immigration enriches German sport. One of the programme's focal areas is working with groups which have previously been under-represented in sport, for example girls and women. Together with the "Bundesliga-Stiftung" and the German Football Association, the Federal Government has also launched an integration initiative. This finances projects for integrating refugees in sport. The project "1:0 für ein Willkommen" – 1:0 for a Welcome, which the German national team supports, and its continuation "2:0 für ein Willkommen" have since 2015 provided financial assistance to some 3,400 clubs that work with refugees on a voluntary basis. ▸

MILESTONES

1954
Germany wins the World Cup for the first time in Switzerland (beating Hungary 3:2 in the final). The "Miracle of Bern" becomes a lasting symbol of post-War Germany.

1972
The Olympic Games in Munich are overshadowed by Israeli athletes being taken hostage and murdered by Palestinian terrorists.

1988
Steffi Graf becomes the first female tennis player to win the Golden Slam, i.e., all four Grand Slam tournaments plus an Olympic Gold medal, in a single calendar year.

At the 2018 PyeongChang Paralympics, monoskier Anna Schaffelhuber won two Gold medals

2006

With its official motto "A Time To Make Friends", the World Cup becomes an unforgettable "summer fairy tale" and puts Germany in a highly favourable light abroad.

2014

Having shone throughout the tournament in Brazil, the German football team once again becomes World Champion (beating Argentina 1:0 in the final). It is Germany's fourth World Cup title since 1954.

2018

Figure skaters Aljona Savchenko and Bruno Massot win Olympic Gold and the World Championships in pairs skating for Germany – both with a world record in the free programme.

The German Olympic Sports Confederation is an umbrella organisation for German sport and sees itself as Germany's largest civic group. It promotes top-class and grassroots sport. More than 20,000 of the 91,000 sports clubs it represents were founded after German Reunification in 1990. Founded in 1900, the German Football Association is also one of the 98 member organisations. The seven million members in 25,000 football clubs represent an all-time high in the Association's history, and it is the world's largest national sports association.

Alongside sport climbing, modern pentathlon, and boxing, one of the sports with the most new members is triathlon. Club membership more than doubled between 2001 and 2015. In 2017, almost 85,000 men and women were active in this sport.

The Bundesliga, the top-flight league in German football, is the shining light in German sport. Internationally it is regarded as one of the strongest leagues. In the 2016-7 season, the 306 matches played between the 18 Bundesliga teams were watched live in the stadiums by around 12.7 million spectators, an average of 41,500 per game. Bayern Munich is the measure of all things in German club football. In April 2018 the club won the German championship for the 28th time, on top of which it has lifted the German Football Association Cup 18 times, and in 2001 and 2013 was victorious in the Champions League. With more than 290,000 members, it is the club with the most members in the world.

The German men's team has won the World Cup four times and the European Championships on three occasions, and is

63,000+ runners: The J.P. Morgan Corporate Challenge in Frankfurt is the biggest road race of its kind in the world

the flagship of German football. Having won the 2014 World Cup in Brazil, Germany heads the FIFA World Rankings. Trained by Joachim Löw, the team is considered to be tactically flexible, and stands for a modern interpretation of the game. The national team squad includes several players with a migratory background, such as Jérôme Boateng, Sami Khedira, and Mesut Özil.

Sporting recognition and success in various disciplines

Alongside football, popular sports are gymnastics, tennis, shooting, athletics, handball, and riding. But other sporting events are also highly successful, for example the J. P. Morgan Corporate Challenge in Frankfurt am Main. Raced by some 63,000 participants from 2,419 companies, the corporate charity run is regarded as the biggest event of its kind in the world.

German sport is a success story in many respects. This is also thanks to the promotion of sport by Stiftung Deutsche Sporthilfe. It supports around 4,000 athletes from almost all Olympic disciplines, traditional non-Olympic sports, as well as sports for disabled and deaf people. Supporting athletes who have disabilities is likewise an important aspect. And here too, having now won a total of 1,871 medals (2018), athletes from Germany have been highly successful at international competitions and the Paralympic Games.

The International Sports Promotion programme of the Federal Foreign Office is a firm part of its cultural relations and education activities abroad, and has already supported more than 1,400 short and long-term projects in various sports in over 100 countries. One example is a long-term project promoting women's football in Uruguay, which trains female coaches and enables women and girls better access to sport, particularly football.

In this and many other ways, German sport is striving to reach levels of excellence as a means of crisis prevention and understanding between peoples, and as an ambassador for more fairness, tolerance, integration, peaceful competition, and performance. ■

GLOBAL

Anti-Doping Initiatives

With the founding of the World Anti-Doping Agency (WADA) in 1999 and the commitment of all stakeholders to a zero-tolerance policy towards doping, the need arose for a uniform set of rules that applied world-wide. This was implemented for the first time in 2003 with the foundation of the World Anti-Doping Code (WADC) and updated in 2015. A new version is due to come into force on 1 January 2021.

→ wada-ama.org

PANORAMA

ATTRACTIONS IN BERLIN

Mitte

Friedrichshain-
Kreuzberg

Berlin Districts

A. Mitte
B. Friedrichshain-Kreuzberg
C. Pankow
D. Charlottenburg-Wilmersdorf
E. Spandau
F. Steglitz-Zehlendorf
G. Tempelhof-Schöneberg
H. Neukölln
I. Treptow-Köpenick
J. Marzahn-Hellersdorf
K. Lichtenberg
L. Reinickendorf

❶ Kaiser Wilhelm Memorial Church
Off Kurfürstendamm, the landmark of western downtown, an anti-war memorial.

❷ Victory Column
There are 285 steps up to the viewing platform, from where there is a fantastic view of the city.

❸ Reichstag Building
Home of the Deutscher Bundestag, the German parliament. The glass dome is a real magnet for visitors.

3,712,000
inhabitants

12,970,000
tourists

2,300,000
visitors to Museum Island

175
museums and collections

❹ Brandenburg Gate
Every Berlin tourist knows the Brandenburg Gate, the symbol of German Reunification.

❺ Potsdamer Platz
The face of modern Berlin. The complex was developed after the fall of the Wall on an enormous piece of waste land.

❻ Gendarmenmarkt
One of the most beautiful squares in Europe boasts no less than three Classicist-style monumental structures.

❼ Checkpoint Charlie
The Wall is no longer, but the former military checkpoint still rekindles memories of the Cold War.

❽ Museum Island
The five major museums house some of Europe's finest collections.

❾ TV Tower on Alexanderplatz
Berlin's TV Tower on the "Alex" can be seen from afar, and from the sphere there is a view of the entire region.

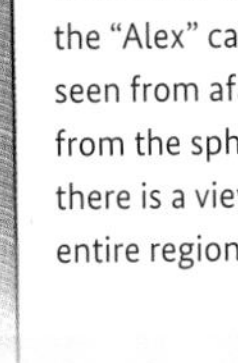

❿ East Side Gallery
The elaborately painted remains of the Wall are nowadays the world's longest open-air gallery.

496,471
visitors to the Berlin Film Festival

4,500,000
visitors to the zoo

4,660
restaurants

402
bars and discotheques

TOPIC

LEISURELY ENJOYMENT

Since the beginning of the millennium, German wine has seen a veritable renaissance internationally, which has much to do with the term "Riesling miracle" and is to a large extent embodied by a young generation of vintners who focus more on high quality than high profits. The long growing season and comparatively low summer heat ensure German wines are refined and do not have a high alcohol content.

German wines are grown in 13 areas in which, across a gross area of around 102,000 hectares, a large variety of wines typical of each particular region are produced. Given the amount of land used, and a grand total of about 80,000 vineyards, Germany is, compared with other countries, one of the medium-sized wine-producing nations; in 2017 production stood at 8.1 million hectolitres. Organic wine has a market share of between four and five percent. The German wine growing areas are some of the most northerly in the world. Apart from Saxony and Saale-Unstrut they are primarily located in the south and southwest of the country. The three biggest growing areas are Rhinehessen, the Palatinate, and Baden. Almost 140 types of grape are grown, whereby some two dozen are of major significance for the market, primarily the white Riesling and Müller-Thurgau varieties. There is a split of about 64 percent white wine and 36 percent red wine, whereby pinot noir and Dornfelder are the most important varieties of red grape.

NUMBER

300

restaurants in Germany, more than ever before, were awarded one, two, or even three Guide Michelin stars in 2018. Eleven restaurants were include in the top 3-star category. Germany thus maintained its position as the European country with the most 3-star establishments after France, the country of gourmets.

→ **bookatable.com/de/guide-michelin**

Germany is also a beer-loving country. German beer is appreciated primarily on account of what is in some cases a centuries-old brewing tradition practised by small family and monastery breweries. The Beer Purity Law of 1516, the world's oldest food law, applies to all German beers without exception. It states that apart from water, hops, and barley, no other ingredients may be used. Between 5,000 and 6,000 sorts of beer are produced in Germany, most of them are Pilsner beers; overall, however, consumption is falling.

There is no clear picture for eating habits in Germany. On the one hand, many consumers

Big-city flair: In Berlin, as well as in other German cities, there is a lively restaurant scene

are becoming increasingly health and fitness-conscious, and are opting for balanced nutritional concepts. On the other, megatrends such as mobility and the ever greater number of different personal lifestyles are clearly influencing eating and drinking habits.

The German restaurant scene is as vibrant as it is diverse – and is one of the best in Europe. Alongside top-class, fusion cuisine, and chefs increasingly catering to vegetarian and vegan dishes; old vegetable varieties such as parsnip, turnip, and Jerusalem artichoke are enjoying a renaissance. They are the pillars of the current boom in all things healthy, seasonal, regional, and the taste of home regions. A young generation of chefs is reinterpreting classic dishes and spicing them up with global influences. ■

PICTURE CREDITS

Cover	querbeet/Getty Images; Anita Back/laif
p. 3	drbimages/Getty Images
p. 4	Westend61/Getty Images
p. 16	Jesco Denzel/Bundesregierung; Steffen Kugler/Bundesregierung; Jörg Carstensen/dpa; Bundesverfassungsgericht
p. 18	picture-alliance/Bernd von Jutrczenka
p. 19	Bundesregierung (19)
p. 20	DB Stiftung Weimarer Klassik/dpa; picture-alliance/arkivi; http://www.jsbach.net/bass/elements/bach-hausmann.jpg. Lizenziert unter Gemeinfrei über Wikimedia Commons - https://commons.wikimedia.org
p. 21	picture-alliance/akg-images; picture-alliance/akg-images/Beethovenhaus Bonn; Buddenbrookhaus Lübeck; picture-alliance/akg-images/Erich Lessing; picture-alliance/dpa; picture-alliance/Thomas Muncke
p. 23	picture-alliance/Daniel Kalker; ullstein bild - Boness/IPON
p. 24	Steffen Kugler/Bundesregierung/dpa
p. 25	Soeren Stache/dpa
p. 27	Nikada/Getty Images
p. 31	RONNY HARTMANN/AFP/Getty Images
p. 33	David Baltzer/Zenit/laif
pp. 34 – 35	Einhorn Solutions
p. 39	Westend 61; Tim Brakemeier/dpa
p. 40	picture-alliance/Wiktor Dabkowski
p. 41	picture-alliance/Kay Nietfeld
p. 44	2013 Bundeswehr/Bier
p. 49	picture-alliance/Photoshot
p. 51	EPA/VALENTIN FLAURAUD
pp. 54 – 55	Einhorn Solutions
p. 57	Joerg Boethling
p. 59	Ole Spata/dpa; Franz Bischof/laif
p. 60	Frank Rumpenhorst/dpa
p. 61	Jan Woitas/dpa
p. 63	Jörg Modrow/laif
p. 65	picture-alliance/Geisler-Fotopress
p. 67	Alexander Koerner/Getty Images
p. 71	Thomas Köhler/Photothek via Getty Images
p. 73	The New York Times/Redux/laif
pp. 74 – 75	Einhorn Solutions
p. 77	Ute Grabowsky/Photothek via Getty Images
p. 79	Frank Krahmer/Photographer's Choice; Matthias Balk/dpa
p. 80	picture-alliance/Keystone
p. 81	Angelika Warmuth/dpa
p. 83	Oliver Berg/dpa
p. 85	Krisztian Bocsi/Bloomberg via Getty Images
p. 89	Uwe Anspach/dpa
pp. 90 – 91	Einhorn Solutions
p. 95	Wolfgang Stahr/laif; David Fischer/dpa
p. 96	Andreas Rentz/Getty Images
p. 99	impress picture/ullsteinbild
p. 103	Thomas Ernsting/laif
p. 107	Thomas Koehler/Photothek via Getty Images
p. 109	DAAD/Konstantin Gastmann
pp. 110 – 111	Einhorn Solutions
p. 113	Thomas Trutschel/Photothek via Getty Images
p. 115	Altrendo Images; Thomas Kierok/laif
p. 116	Gregor Hohenberg/laif
p. 117	Andrea Enderlein
p. 119	Martin Stoever/Bongarts/Getty Images
p. 123	Sean Gallup/Getty Images
p. 124	Michael Löwa/dpa
p. 127	picture-alliance/Andreas Franke
p. 129	Thomas Lohnes/Getty Images
pp. 130 – 131	Einhorn Solutions
p. 133	Boris Roessler/dpa
p. 135	HILMER & SATTLER und ALBRECHT – Jan Pautzke; Janetzko/Berlinale 2013
p. 136	Arno Burgi/dpa
p. 137	Rainer Jensen/dpa
p. 139	Marko Priske/laif
p. 141	picture-alliance/abacapress
p. 143	picture-alliance/Eventpress Hoensch
p. 144	picture-alliance/ZUMA Press
p. 147	Malte Christians/dpa
p. 148	Tim Brakemeier/dpa
pp. 150 – 151	Einhorn Solutions
p. 153	Goethe-Institut/Anastasia Tsayder/dpa
p. 155	Sabine Lubenow/Getty Images; Dagmar Schwelle/laif
p. 156	Dagmar Schwelle/laif
p. 157	Daniel Biskup/laif
p. 159	Thomas Linkel/laif
p. 161	Christian Kerber/laif
p. 165	picture-alliance/Alexandra Wey/KEYSTONE
p. 166	Christoph Schmidt/dpa
pp. 168 – 169	Einhorn Solutions
p. 171	Georg Knoll/laif

INDEX

IMPRINT

Publisher
FAZIT Communication GmbH, Frankfurt am Main, in cooperation with the German Federal Foreign Office, Berlin

Concept and Chief Editors
Peter Hintereder, Janet Schayan
Editors
Johannes Göbel, Martin Orth, Dr. Helen Sibum
Authors
Matthias Bischoff, Dr. Eric Chauvistré,
Constanze Kleis, Joachim Wille
Art direction
Martin Gorka
Panorama info graphics
Einhorn Solutions
Production
Kerim Demir, André Herzog

Translations
Dr. Jeremy Gaines

FAZIT Communication GmbH
Frankenallee 71–81
60327 Frankfurt am Main, Germany
Internet: www.fazit-communication.de
Email: tatsachen@fazit-communication.de

Federal Foreign Office
Directorate-General for Culture and Communication
Werderscher Markt 1
10117 Berlin, Germany
Internet: www.auswaertiges-amt.de
Email: 608-R@auswaertiges-amt.de

Printing
Krüger Druck+Verlag GmbH & Co. KG
66763 Dillingen, Germany
Printed in Germany 2018

Deadline for copy
June 2018
ISBN
978-3-96251-032-9

“Facts about Germany”
is published in the following languages
Arabic, Chinese, English, French, German, Indonesian, Japanese, Korean, Polish, Portuguese, Russian, Spanish, Turkish and Ukrainian

“Facts about Germany” online
www.facts-about-germany.de